The Teaching of Ethics III

Teaching Ethics in Journalism Education

Clifford G. Christians
Catherine L. Covert

The Hastings Center
Institute of Society, Ethics and the Life Sciences
360 Broadway
Hastings-on-Hudson, New York 10706

Library of Congress Cataloging in Publication Data

Christians, Clifford G
    Teaching ethics in journalism education.

    (The Teaching of ethics ; 3)
    Bibliography: p.
    1. Journalistic ethics—Study and teaching.
I. Covert, Catherine L., joint author. II. Title.
III. Series: Teaching of ethics ; 3.
PN4756.C47   174'.9097   80–10426
ISBN 0–916558–08–8

Printed in the United States of America

Contents

Introduction ix

I. HISTORICAL BACKGROUND 1
   A. Journalism Education 1
   B. Journalism Profession 6

II. STATE-OF-THE-ART IN ETHICS INSTRUCTION .. 11
   A. Schools With Ethics Courses 11
   B. Schools Without Ethics Courses 13
   C. Textbook Material Used 15
   D. Pedagogical Techniques 16
   E. Observations 16

III. SUBSTANTIVE ISSUES IN MEDIA ETHICS
   COURSES 25
   A. Content of Courses in Journalism Ethics 25
   B. Issues Shared With Professional Education Gener-
      ally 28
      1. Community 28
      2. Truthfulness 30
      3. Paternalism 31
      4. Whistle-blowing 32
   C. Issues Resulting From Historical Circumstance ... 33
      1. Codes 33
      2. Adversarity 34
   D. Implications 35

IV. INSTRUCTIONAL OBJECTIVES 37
    A. Recognizing Ethical Issues.................... 38
    B. Developing Analytical Skills 38
    C. Stimulating The Moral Imagination 40
    D. Eliciting Moral Obligation 43
    E. Summary 45

V. MAJOR INTELLECTUAL CONCERN 49

VI. RECOMMENDATIONS......................... 53
    A. Overall Planning 53
    B. Research 53
    C. Teaching................................. 54
    D. Relations With Practitioners................. 56

NOTES 59

BIBLIOGRAPHY 67

FOREWORD

A concern for the ethical instruction and formation of students has always been a part of American higher education. Yet that concern has by no means been uniform or free of controversy. The centrality of moral philosophy in the undergraduate curriculum during the mid-nineteenth century gave way later during that century to the first signs of increasing specialization of the disciplines. By the middle of the twentieth century, instruction in ethics had, by and large, become confined almost exclusively to departments of philosophy and religion. Efforts to introduce ethics teaching in the professional schools and elsewhere in the university often met with indifference or outright hostility.

The past decade has seen a remarkable resurgence of interest in the teaching of ethics at both the undergraduate and professional school levels. Beginning in 1977, The Hastings Center, with the support of the Rockefeller Brothers Fund and the Carnegie Corporation of New York, undertook a systematic study of the teaching of ethics in American higher education. Our concern focused on the extent and quality of that teaching, and on the main possibilities and problems posed by widespread efforts to find a more central and significant role for ethics in the curriculum.

As part of that project, a number of papers, studies, and monographs were commissioned. Moreover, in an attempt to gain some degree of consensus, the authors of those studies worked together as a group for a period of two years. The study presented here represents one outcome of the project. We hope and believe it will be helpful for those concerned to advance and deepen the teaching of ethics in higher education.

Daniel Callahan   Sissela Bok
Project Co-Directors
The Hastings Center
Project on the Teaching of Ethics

About the Authors

Clifford Glenn Christians

Clifford Glenn Christians teaches media ethics and the social philosophy of communications at the College of Communications, University of Illinois-Urbana. In addition to his training in the classics, sociolinguistics, and communications (PH.D., Illinois), he has two graduate degrees in theology. He was recently a Visiting Fellow in Philosophy at Princeton University. He has co-authored (with William Rivers and Wilbur Schramm) *Responsibility in Mass Communication* and with Jay Van Hook, *Jacques Ellul: Interpretive Essays*.

Catherine L. Covert

Catherine L. Covert is Professor of Journalism at the Newhouse School of Public Communications, Syracuse University. She received her B.A. in journalism from the University of Iowa and her Ph.D. from Syracuse University in American Intellectual History. She is the recipient of the Lasker Award and the Blakeslee Award for her professional work in science writing for the mass media. Her scholarly interests lie in the history of scientific idea transmission in mass media and in the cultural foundations of professionalism, particularly ethics, history, sociology, and the arts.

Introduction

Journalism's role in public and private life is highly controversial today. The mass media have been grouped by reflective social critics with computer technology, the conquest of space, and splitting the atom as major agents of contemporary change.[1] No longer the independent entrepreneurs of colonial days, media professionals are increasingly situated within a complex corporate structure. Such a position produces fresh dilemmas in the balancing of personal, social, and corporate responsibility. Now frequently challenged from outside by the courts, journalists are also more and more concerned about the legal position of the profession, recognizing at the same time that legally defined responsibilities are only a point of departure for larger questions of media morality.

Journalism is only one of several vocations that senses a rising critical reaction from the public. Many issues that concern journalism trouble other professions as well—issues of credibility, confidentiality, paternalism, among others. As part of a cooperative inquiry into the teaching of professional ethics, this monograph has been completed in connection with The Hastings Center Project on the Teaching of Ethics supported by a grant from the Carnegie Corporation of New York.

In preparing this study, the reflections of a representative group of professionals and educators have been incorporated, and the experiences of ethics teachers in schools of journalism across the country utilized.[2] Introduced into journalism classrooms in the first decades of this century, the study of moral problems has continued for the past fifty years in various guises including courses devoted to "professional responsibility" or to the broader concerns of mass media and society. Now the focus seems in many places to be locating once again around specific attention to ethics in separate courses. This study assesses that trend.

Focusing on the education of journalists who will be engaged in newsgathering, either for print or the electronic media, we consider first the development historically of news reporting and of journalism education in reference to matters of ethics. In the second section we discuss the state of the art in media ethics instruction; in the third, substantive issues in ethics courses; in the fourth, instructional objectives. A major intellectual concern is outlined in conclusion, and a set of recommendations proposed for further discussion and future action.

I. Historical Background

Two historical streams—one shaping journalism education and the other molding the journalism profession—have produced the quality and scope of ethics instruction that characterize media education today.

A. Journalism Education

Schools of journalism were first established in the early decades of the twentieth century. By that time, news reporting of various kinds had flourished on this continent for two hundred years, and apprenticeship training had been the educational mode. Then, in 1903, Joseph Pulitzer announced a major endowment to Columbia University for creating a School of Journalism. The logic of professional education had been debated vigorously since Congress had authorized land-grant universities in 1862; journalism emerged in the academic world along with the surge of professional education that followed the Morrill Act.[3] But it was Pulitzer's initiative that helped precipitate a shift from informal learning in the printer's shop to formal instruction within the university.

The first generation of journalism educators was inspired by the Progressive Era, in fact by a particular brand of progressivism linked to the moralistic perspective of the small town (a tradition, as Richard Hofstader notes, inherited largely from rural evangelical Protestantism).[4] Given these small-town, often midwestern roots, it is not surprising that many early schools of journalism—except for those with particular origins such as Columbia—were founded in the Midwest (Illinois, 1904; Wisconsin, 1905; Missouri, 1908; and Northwestern, 1921, for example).

Much of the *rhetoric* from journalism educators during the teens and twenties was couched in religious terms, sought high-mindedness, decried sensationalism, and encouraged social reform. But the *work* of these early educators indicates that explicit progressive values swiftly became less significant than the dignity and status of journalism itself. Such educators consistently promoted the idea of professionalism as a mode for achieving acceptance and recognition. The *Journalism Bulletin*, founded in 1924 as the voice of collegiate journalism educators, and its successor, the *Journalism Quarterly*, carried an extended argument on behalf of formal education and codes as two avenues for turning journalism into a full-scale, honorable, legitimate profession.

The problem of a proper definition for "professionalism" and the question as to whether journalism qualified for admission to formal professional status continued to be controversial during the twenties, even as it is until today; the ongoing debate tended to focus attention in schools of journalism on journalism's status and on the definition of appropriate modes of judgment and behavior for practitioners.[5]

First-generation educators solved the problem for their decades by comparing journalism to law and medicine as a public trust, seeking for their occupation a professional status equal to that of those more venerable fields. Joseph Pulitzer echoed this rhetoric specifically. Nearly all the material on journalism education published between 1903 and 1930, in fact, mentions law and medicine. By imitating their preoccupation with codes, licensing, and formal education, it was assumed, journalism could best achieve an equivalent professional status. Thus, Frank Scott, the first man to teach journalism courses at the University of Illinois, argued in 1924: "Establishing a firm professional standing requires the creation of a generally accepted ethics code...so that the charlatan in journalism will take his place with the shyster [in law] and the quack [in medicine]."[6] And E. M. Johnson of Minnesota constantly lamented unserious "jazz journalism" and sought through education the "scientific news experts" who could lift journalists above what he believed to be their frequently perceived role as "entertainers."[7] Upgrading "the profession's honor" became a common rationale for media education, considered as vital as the need to teach reportorial competence.[8]

However, as journalism education developed, the model of law and medicine proved inappropriate for a constitutionally protected process rooted in a profit-making enterprise. In its development to a position of power in American society, journalism came more to resemble a public utility in its goals of public service and profit. Later in the twentieth century, with the development of radio and television journalism, the third attribute of a public utility (government regulation) became accepted and legitimated. The entrenched position of print journalism, based on First Amendment rights, provided a restraining influence against such political supervision. However, twin enterprises eventually developed in the twentieth century—journalism in the form of print as *unregulated* commercial enterprise providing news both as public service and commodity, and journalism in the form of electronic broadcasting offered as a *regulated* public service within the economic framework.

But even before this creature had fully taken shape, the traditional forms of codes and licensing proved inappropriate. Codes seemed to interfere with First Amendment protection of free expression, and licensing applied only to broadcasting, but in the form of licensing stations, not individual practitioners.

Appropriate perhaps to the nature of its undertaking, journalism has not developed a body of tightly organized professionals in single societies controlling the supply of entrants to the field through formal educational requirements and licensing. As a literary art based on a talent rather generally distributed throughout the population, journalism involves a basic skill with the language, a talent not restricted to graduates of approved schools of instruction. From the beginning, formal requirements in this regard have been difficult to enforce.

Neither has journalism ever developed formal procedures for self-policing. Rather, a varied group of professional societies has emerged around various aspects of journalistic practice—editing, publishing, broadcasting, reporting—and these joined in a national accrediting body (American Council on Education for Journalism) which sets broad principles rather than more narrowly specific qualifications for journalism education. Some of these groups developed codes, which served more as idealized statements on attitude and performance than as enforced mechanisms for regulating conduct. Ethical behavior was policed rather by peer action on the basis of information transmitted via informal networks of communication. Ostracism from the group, dismissal, failure to hire—all these were sanctions employed in the interests of social control (somewhat as failure to refer became a controlling mechanism, informal but effective, in medicine).[9]

It is possible that this failure to develop single economically and politically powerful professional groups had stemmed in part from the crucial separation in the mid-nineteenth century of the original editor-publisher function; editors became employees of publishers who owned and controlled journalistic enterprises and work places. Though publishers frequently honored the social responsibilities commensurate with the nature of the news undertaking, news personnel themselves did not control their work places as did the clergy, lawyers, and doctors who set the rules for procedure in churches, law courts, and hospitals. Journalists as professionals became subordinates within organizations, developing informal and irregularly applied sanctions against unethical deportment (particularly when resolving conflicts of interest).

Professionals also exerted indirect rather than direct influence over professional education which emerged in a pattern quite different from that for law and medicine. This lack of formal controls perhaps served to make journalism education more immediately responsive to educational fashion than to specified professional demands. Educators assumed as a model in the 1920s the individual broadly educated in the arts and sciences and enabled by special skills in communication to transmit to others a liberally informed understanding of the world. Three-fourths of course work was to be outside journalism. This large proportion of substantive courses was justified by the rationale that art, science, politics, and religion would be the stuff of which journalistic reporting would be made (though political science figures largely in the curriculum as an aid to embryonic journalists in their potential political roles as government watchdogs). The desirable individual was also to be shaped by a one-fourth mixture of professional courses in entry-level skills, together with some liberal courses with specific professional applications—the history of the profession, the ethics of the profession, and so forth.

There were departures from the liberal ideal. Those schools that took on a trade-school atmosphere emphasized skills courses, paid little attention to academic qualifications of those teaching media law, ethics, or history, and less to any coherent organization of the liberal arts curriculum outside the journalism school. By midcentury, some schools striving to be more than technical training centers had organized their professional curricula around the fashionable social sciences. The procedures of the statistician and the paradigm of objectivity dominated these programs. Influenced by the prominence of political and social science, courses in ethics drew more and more heavily on political theory and often were retitled as courses in professional responsibility. Such courses focused primarily on the journalist's political and social responsibilities at an organizational level and tended to stint the more immediate dilemmas of individual decisionmaking. Generally, throughout journalism education from the thirties on, the teaching of reporting and editing was subtly influenced in its perspectives by the positivistic tenets so influential in professional education everywhere during the central decades of the century. The journalist's major ethical imperative was to remain value-free.

Two separate educational patterns evolved. The most common was that of a four-year curriculum of undergraduate courses of which three-fourths were to be in the arts and sciences and not more than one-fourth in specifically professional courses. This requirement was formalized through national accrediting standards established in 1946. Such standards were designed to prevent workshop courses from dominating the curriculum and to protect against the cramping of a broader humanist perspective for which medicine particularly was criticized as the century evolved.

An alternative path offered by such schools as Northwestern and Columbia was that of a one-year master's program, admitting to professional education only those with a baccalaureate degree and focusing on professional courses. Many schools began offering both bachelor's and master's degrees. Journalism education resembled something of the variety characterizing schools of engineering in the same period. Journalists came to be regarded as professionally educated whether they held bachelor's or master's degrees in journalism or both. Journalism degrees became increasingly important credentials, however; graduates in the field competed with a dwindling number of those without college degrees. But also hired were those boasting degrees in unrelated fields who had decided they wished to become journalists.

As to specific education in ethics within the journalism program, a lively debate flourished between 1903 and 1930. Some lamented the whole trend toward professionalism and worried, as Emile Durkheim did, about the shift from community life to vocations. Four worthwhile texts appeared, all connecting themselves to ethics as an academic pursuit with ancient roots. As the 1930s moved forward, the rhetoric about professional status continued as well. The ambiguous dual nature of undergraduate and graduate education for journalism became accepted too. Now for several decades the debate went silent. Courses once titled "Principles of Journalism" were retitled "Mass Media and Society," reflecting not only the increasingly perceived power of journalism, but the fashionable shift toward political and social science as an interpretive framework. Emphasis turned from individual ethical decisions to organizational responsibilities toward society as a whole. Two new ethics textbooks—one in 1957, another in 1963—reflected this trend. In the later seventies came several more texts. The increasingly important ethical debate in the profession and in the educational fraternity (after Watergate), began to reflect a return to concerns for individual decisionmaking and attempts to base professional choice on more systematic approaches to ethical thinking.

B. Journalism Profession

In addition to influences from within educational circles, approaches to ethics courses have been strongly if indirectly influenced by the values that have developed in the profession. Accumulated over a long historical period, these values (defined minimally as preferred attitudes and behaviors) have been transmitted informally but continuously from newsroom to classroom and condition the ethos in which media ethics courses are designed and promoted. What are the traditional newsroom expectations as to style and goal of performance?

In the classic concept of the newsroom the premium goes to the macho virtues—toughness, skepticism, enterprise, competitiveness. The valued person is the individualist—detached, self-contained, unruffled—with a sort of wry wit to gloss over the crises of the newsroom day. Overtly, at least, there is a premium on rapid decision rather than on extended deliberation, on response rather than reflection. The person of action is valued; the intellectual is frequently suspect. Most displays of emotion are considered effete. Such a listing of qualities represents the stereotype, and many professionals today evidence greater sensitivity and reserve. Nonetheless, this stark delineation of the traditional pattern evokes the essence of what is still the dominant newsroom value system. It did not come out of a vacuum—the qualities are as evolved as Darwin's finches to meet real and pressing environmental demands.

Relevant aspects of this newsroom culture stem first from the relationship of journalism to the craft of printing, second from its place in an economic enterprise, and third from the journalist's role as political advocate in the colonial period and the early days of the Republic.[10]

The relationship of journalists to "craft" has exposed them historically to the limitations and opportunities of increasingly sophisticated technology. The tendency with such new technology, from the Washington press to satellites, has frequently been to convert an "is" to a "should," to assume that because any tempo or mode of news distribution has become technologically *possible,* that it should be put into effect. The prospective impact on news, newsmen, or potential audience has rarely been given more than a superficial advance look. Deadline pressures have always been enormous, but the rapidity of transmission today makes even more demands for increased speed by journalists. As noted later, this technological development has bounded the newsman's concept of social and ethical responsibilities in powerful, if unanticipated, fashion.

Second, the position of the journalist as businessman-printer in colonial days and then as newspaper editor-publisher in the early

Republic placed him within an enterprise which packaged and sold a consumer product consisting of information, persuasion, and entertainment. By the mid-nineteenth century, the editorial function was being separated from that of owning-publishing, that of newsman from that of financier. Since then, a majority of journalists engaged in daily newsgathering has occupied positions as employees of major corporations. Such journalists have experienced increasing dissonance in attempting to reconcile their responsibilities as newsgatherers with the objectives of an economic structure designed primarily for profit.[11]

Third, the American journalist's role after the Revolution as the hired voice of one political party made him vulnerable to political pressure. This experience sensitized him to the potential of unfriendly parties in power interfering with publication. In the two centuries following the Revolution, newspapers as institutions increasingly withdrew themselves from overt affiliation with any one party and tried increasingly to provide "objective" versions of reality. But, it may be argued, early vulnerability to government pressure helped to focus journalists' attention on their right to *publish,* regardless of consequence, and to pay commensurately less attention to social or ethical reasons why they should, on specific occasions, find reason *not* to publish. Virtue lay in the action, not in the refraining from action and not in considering consequences. Providing the news, uncensored, became their aim.

Demands for fulfillment of these three historic roles have been accompanied by a performance demand for physical and psychological conquest of the environment. Journalists must meet and encompass a vast, ambiguous scene; they must be able to impose themselves physically on events, confront personal danger, maintain detachment in the face of suffering, continue to function in chaos. They are expected to extract information from the recalcitrant, knock demandingly on the doors of the resistant, continue in the face of refusal and disdain. Methods for "routinizing the unexpected" have succeeded in producing calm and orderly newsrooms, and most journalists have developed the tough outer shell necessary to preserve personal tranquillity in the face of crisis and urgency.[12] But the qualities for meeting extraordinary expectations have become, nonetheless, a part of the journalist's behavioral and attitudinal repertoire. Richard Harding Davis and Ernest Hemingway still lurk somewhere offstage in the romantic imagery of the trade, with Robert Woodward and Carl Bernstein as more pallid but still persuasive recent exemplars. Aggressive attitudes are effectively expressed in newsroom rhetoric—the value on "hard" rather than "soft" news, and on "getting the story" as the primary demand.

These newsroom values enter and condition journalism classrooms through several informal channels. The first route is via the early socialization of the professoriat. Professional experience in the newsroom is a common prerequisite for faculty appointment; those who elect the graduate school route as a primary path to teaching also most commonly must demonstrate professional qualifications. Thus a significant number of faculty members have been socialized at a vital early point in their adult years to newsroom patterns of thinking and action. They share and embody many professional values.[13] A second factor comes through the expectations of those in the news industry, exerted on the classroom through the presence of professionals as visiting members of faculties, as potential employers, and as participants in accrediting bodies. Less directly there are corporate grants to education, and the close association of professionals with journalism administrators and faculty members in organizations of editors, publishers, reporters, and broadcasters.

A dissonance thus arises between conflicting ideas as to the primary purpose of professional education. On the one hand is the common assumption that the major objective of a professional school is to prepare students to meet professional demands as they exist in the field and to socialize them to contemporary standards and values. The opposing idea is that students should be educated as critics of accepted attitudes and practices—in effect, as bearers of antiestablishment values. In this way, goes the second view, can the professional school realize its primary purpose as exemplar for the field at large.[14]

The issue must be faced more directly, perhaps, in the ethics classroom than anywhere else in the school. Whatever the conflicting philosophies of education, the practitioner's presence is omnipresent in the school, expressed in subtle as well as overt ways. It heavily influences what is considered by typical faculty, administrators, and aspiring journalists to be an acceptable course in media ethics. In fashioning educational goals and designing curricula, the challenge—while taking these expectations seriously—is to find ways for healthy individual decisionmaking to prosper within such a highly pressurized environment. Broadly speaking, until recently the history of journalism education and the development of journalism's professional character have militated against an interest in formal ethics instruction, and have favored instead more generalized courses in institutional responsibility to government and society.

II. State-of-the-art in Ethics Instruction

Given that historical context, what one sees in the media ethics curriculum at present is only symptomatic of these long-running currents, with ethics teaching illustrative in turn of several dynamics throughout journalism education as a whole. A 1977 survey ascertained the current state-of-the-art in teaching media ethics and makes this general conclusion more specific. It was designed to identify actual ethics courses in news-editorial programs (both print and broadcasting) and to delineate their primary features.[15]

A. Schools With Ethics Courses

As noted in Table 1, 27 percent of the 237 schools that responded teach a specific course in ethics. Some nonaccredited schools have only limited sequences, making separate ethics instruction physically impossible. The overall quality and range connected with graduate programs is reflected in a higher percentage (48 percent) of ethics courses offered. However, in general terms, factors of size and accreditation did not influence the percentages substantially.

TABLE 1

Schools With Specific Ethics Courses

	Total Schools	No. with Courses	Pct. with Courses
Nonaccredited schools ..	170	43	25%
Accredited schools	67	23	34%
Schools with 500 or more majors	42	15	33%
Schools with 50 or more grad students	39	19	48%
All schools	237	66	27%

Most schools offering a special course in ethics require it for their students, present it on the undergraduate level, and teach it every semester. A further breakdown of these curricular matters appears in Table 2.[16]

TABLE 2

Ethics Course's Place in Curriculum
(64 of 66 Schools Responding)

	No.	Pct.
Status for degree:		
Elective	23	36%
Required	38	59%
Option to fulfill requirement	3	5%
Class level:		
Undergraduate	42	65%
Graduate	6	10%
Both combined	16	25%
Teaching schedule:		
Every semester or quarter	28	43%
Annually	26	41%
Alternate years	7	11%
Rarely	3	5%

B. Schools Without Ethics Courses

Of the 237 schools responding, 171 (73 percent) do not teach a special course in media ethics. Table 3 indicates their reasons for not offering one.

TABLE 3

Reasons for Not Offering a Course in Ethics

	No. of Schools	Pct.
Ethical issues are discussed as they arise in other courses	150	88%
Small dept. with limited program	24	14%
No good instructional material exists	7	4%
No clear evidence ethics can be taught well in the classroom.................	6	3%
No available room in the curriculum......	6	3%
No qualified person to teach the course ..	4	3%
Handled by the philosophy dept	3	2%
Lack of interest in student body	2	1%
Lack of interest among faculty...........	2	1%

Note: The totals reflect the fact that 21 of the 171 schools checked more than one reason as applicable to their situation.

The conclusion is obvious. About 88 percent of the schools without an ethics course believe it is pedagogically more sound to treat ethical issues as they arise in the classroom. None of the 171 schools argues that ethics are not pertinent to the curriculum. This option was offered in the survey but no one marked it. Twenty-five respondents added explanations or comments at this point, insisting, for example, that "ethics are rooted in the fabric of all media study" and noting that their "faculty feels this is the best approach." Some, in fact, make the case more strongly, suggesting that because their schools feel so intensely about ethics, they insist that students should encounter such issues throughout the curriculum during their entire training. In addition to ethical discussion in the workshop courses, one administrator wrote: "Ethics is of considerable weight in the Mass Media and Society course, Journalism and Contemporary Affairs, Law of the Press, Advertising and Society, Public Relations Problems.'' In a slightly different vein, a few argue that in the ''real world'' ethical questions arise situationally day-by-day; therefore, this is also the most natural way of treating such questions in the classroom.

It should be observed further than 134 of the 150 schools who rely on discussions of ethics throughout the curriculum also have specific chapters or sections devoted to ethics. In those recording actual percentages of time, some schools give 50–70 percent of classroom hours to these ethics units in such courses as ''Journalism in a Free Society.'' Others noted that ethical matters come up ''virtually every day'' in news editing and reporting.

Twenty-four schools said they do not offer courses in ethics because they have limited programs and staffs. A variation on the same theme is the overload of various faculty—''teaching five different courses per year already'' in one instance. Without required graduate-level programs and limited by accreditation from offering more than thirty-six journalism hours, communication schools on the whole find it extremely difficult to include ethics in a curriculum overrun with other demands.

Three schools deliberately encourage or require their students to take ethics from the philosophy department. For example, one such school wrote: ''Our philosophy department offers several excellent ethics courses which many of our majors take. Much of the specifics and the examples used in these courses are taken from contemporary journalism.'' Another said: ''Our core curriculum calls for three courses in philosophy, preferably an ethics course; do we need more, also taught in our department?'' All three are small private colleges with a religious orientation.

Of the 171 schools, ten indicated they plan to offer an ethics course within a year, and six said they have a committee studying its feasibility. One of the ten noted that it thought it was meeting student demand by emphasizing ethics everywhere in the classroom. However, students persuaded the school that this was not sufficient. A specific ethics course is now offered each semester.

C. Textbook Materials Used

A review of the course outlines indicates the varied choices for textbooks in the 64 courses on mass-media ethics.[17] Eight courses require more than one textbook. Of these eight, six combine law and ethics and assign at least one book in each area. One course requires both Hulteng and Merrill-Barney, and another requires both Hulteng and Rivers-Schramm. In the five team-taught courses, one uses the two typical texts (Gross and Merrill-Barney); another assigns Hulteng along with Fletcher's *Situation Ethics*. Otherwise texts are chosen in these courses which are not used in the other 61: John Mill's *On Liberty*, Isaiah Berlin's *Four Essays on Liberty*, Jacques Ellul's *Propaganda*, Henry Thoreau's *Civil Disobedience*, Sinclair Lewis's *Babbit*, Titus and Keeton's *Ethics for Today*.

All the courses require articles in addition to texts, and nine courses use no text at all but articles exclusively. Eight of the nine chose the nontextbook option for three reasons: (a) dissatisfaction with the textbooks available; (b) the flexibility of using articles allows more freedom to structure the course according to personal taste; and (c) texts are quickly out of date (eight correspondents, 13 percent, mentioned this problem), especially for courses based on the case-study approach. One respondent assigns no texts because "they are essentially part of mass culture, the very entity we seek to criticize."

The survey question on textbooks was open-ended, and all respondents used the opportunity to pass judgment on the existing textbook material. Six of the respondents (10 percent) were positive, though not ecstatic. Terms such as "good," "adequate," "generally favorable," "improved in the last few years," "okay," "helpful as springboard to classroom discussion" characterized the evaluations. One response typified the spirit of most: "What we have indicates progress, but available material is barely adequate at present. The market is still new, however, and I hope more challenging texts will soon emerge." An urgent need remains at present for materials with clearly articulated value systems, for books which advance beyond descriptive ethics to self-conscious theoretical frameworks.

D. Pedagogical Techniques Used By Instructors

In an effort to determine how well classroom procedures for teaching ethics are developed, a listing of twenty possible techniques was suggested. The results for the 64 ethics courses are ranked in order of popularity in Table 4.

The most typical procedure appears to be a combination of lectures by instructor, classroom visits by professionals, discussions, and student research papers (with a focus in 45 courses on case studies as the content underlying these procedures). Twenty-one of the 64 (33 percent) do not use any audio-visuals (i.e., tapes, films, overheads, slides, photographs, or clippings).

Several, as noted in Table 5, checked a number of possibilities from the list, the highest being an instructor who uses thirteen of the twenty options and the lowest a course devoted solely to lecture by instructor.

E. Observations

Various assessments follow from this material. These observations emerge from rather complete written survey evidence, but are not enriched by actual observations of all the courses being taught. Thus they are offered to help focus the discussion and better ascertain future direction, but with the preceding disclaimer always in mind.

1. Theoretical frameworks for organizing the material are not fully developed as yet. One searches almost in vain for systematic structures, for clearly articulated value systems, for sets of principles according to which conclusions are drawn. Thus it is a question whether students are enabled to arrive successfully at justified moral judgments. A structure built academically on logical positivism and professionally on the convention of "objective" reporting in which valuing and judging are to be suspended finds it difficult to accommodate value judgments and normative ethics. There is evidence to indicate that ethics teaching is suffering now from several decades of not taking value theory seriously.

The course syllabi, especially the "First Unit" and "Conclu-

TABLE 4

Pedagogical Techniques Used in Ethics Courses

	No. of Courses	Pct.
Lectures by instructor	56	87%
Case studies	45	70%
Small group discussion	36	56%
Student presentations on topics of their own choosing	35	55%
Lectures by outside professionals	34	53%
In-depth study of a few selected issues	28	44%
Panels of opposing viewpoints	20	31%
Students report interviews with professionals	19	29%
Films	15	23%
Audio-tapes	13	20%
Video-tapes	11	17%
Overhead transparencies	11	17%
Slides	10	15%
Sample surveys taken of local media outlets	10	15%
Lectures by academics from other depts. (e.g., philosophy)	10	15%
Role playing	8	12%
Simulation games	3	5%
Novels or plays	1	1%
Clippings	1	1%
Photographs	1	1%

Note: Totals indicate that respondents checked as many as apply.

sion" sections, provided clues that a few courses have perspective. Three or four courses, in fact, offered some intriguing possibilities in their opening sessions, with their section titles indicating a concern for theoretical orientations: "The Nature of Ethical Inquiry," "Foundations and Definitions of Ethics," and "Press Sensationalism as a Historical Problem." One course put the SPJ, SDX Code of Ethics up front as the benchmark by which journalistic practice is to be judged. Two courses made

TABLE 5

No. of Techniques Used in Ethics Courses

Total techniques used	No of classes
13	01
12	01
11	02
10	02
9	03
8	07
7	12
6	09
5	07
4	08
3	08
2	03
1	01
	64 total

objectivity the operating ideal. And as one would expect, the law and ethics courses consistently provided a frame of reference around the First Amendment.

The five courses using Rivers-Schramm's *Responsibility in Mass Communication* exhibit some deliberate structure also. These courses seem much more self-conscious about establishing a theoretical framework, highlighting social responsibility theory as the parameters within which the course proceeds. Since that is the only textbook on media ethics built around a philosophical viewpoint, it is not surprising that the course and book have the same coloration. Two other courses also have a social responsibility framework, one using the Hutchins Commission Report as its basis and another *Four Theories of the Press* (where social responsibility theory is outlined). These seven courses at least might help students think more precisely and provide guidelines by which particular questions can be judged as moral or immoral.

However, that still leaves a large majority of the media ethics courses with apparent weaknesses in their normative posture.

These appear to be collectivities—a potpourri of journalistic practices and problems, a series of scattered ethical snippets—rather than theoretically sophisticated approaches. Not much is included on the nature of ethics and moral reasoning. Aside from five team-taught courses, only one syllabus mentions any moral philosophers past or present; in that case there is no requirement, only an aside: "Read Aristotle and you'll be surprised." In any future exchange of materials among media ethics instructors a description of the theoretical framework employed would be helpful information.

2. Some of the courses may do little more than entrench certain conventions and teach students to appeal to epithets. In these courses, given the choice of subject matter and course organization, it seems very likely that students leave with slogans: "the public's right to know," "adversary relationship," "facts," "First Amendment right to publish," "First Amendment freedom." One syllabus said explicitly, for example: "You will be taught that journalists are free of any obligation other than the people's right to know." On that basis, stolen documents could be defended, as John Harrison contends, almost as though the Ten Commandments were repealed when the First Amendment was ratified.[18] Press performance could then be governed by expediency and improvisation. Minor vices would receive concentration rather than basic moral concepts.

If one distinguishes C-content (formal subject matter) and P-content (the cluster of procedures surrounding the acquisition of knowledge), it is worthy of discussion to consider just what the typical course *process* teaches students.[19] If courses start with First Amendment rights, concentrate on Woodward and Bernstein as exemplars, discuss classic cases as though the press was completely vindicated (Watergate or Pentagon Papers), and constantly attribute importance to the press as the Fourth Estate, does not the course's P-content teach that the press as it presently exists needs no improvement? Is there anything in the process which communicates to students that ethics has a normative bearing, an intellectual scope and substance? Will students be able to provide "whys" to the choices they make? Near-transfers of information will become possible, but what about substantive applications? Will a sense of center and periphery result? In short, will the course expand ethical awareness or undermine it?

There are obvious difficulties here. An insider's perspective is invaluable, and students need concreteness in order to think well. Yet, to the degree that the course's scope becomes narrowly circumscribed and "workshoppish" in tone, to that extent the results might be counterproductive to anything normally meant by instruction in ethics.

3. The intellectual content of these courses tends to be focused more on professional performance than on liberal arts substance. Reflecting the pattern of journalism education at large, the courses are characterized more by matters of form and procedure than by rigorous moral thought. Generally speaking, ethics instruction in journalism schools is not a critical inquiry in a generous educational sense. Once more, the disclaimer above warrants repetition; on-site observation could possibly indicate otherwise. The material in hand, however, prompts the question whether most media ethics courses are really accomplishing more than they could if journalism students only read *Quill, Nieman Reports,* and *Columbia Journalism Review,* all of which provide thoughtful coverage of current press dilemmas. The tendency to reduce other media areas (the "History of Communications" sometimes becomes a name and date listing, for example) seems to happen with media ethics also.

Evidence for the chopping, reducing, and simplifying occurs at several points. In the "Free Press/Fair Trial" section, for instance, one course reduces it to "Resolved: Canon 35, prohibiting cameras in the courtroom, should be repealed." In the section on "Terror and Violence in News," only one course requires even the minimum sociological literature from the federal commissions (Kerner, Eisenhower, Walker, and Surgeon General).

The matter of case studies warrants scrutiny too. Nearly three-fourths of the courses use case studies in various ways and with differing emphases. Half of the courses include local cases ("Indiana Primary," "Iowa Beef," "Idaho Obscenity Laws," for example) and nearly half have at least one classic case (Watergate, Eagleton, Sam Sheppard, Wilbur Mills, Pentagon Papers, Daniel Schorr, Myron Farber). Again, the heavy use of cases appears to raise the question of how instructors get beyond specific situations to basic principles. And other questions deserve consideration: How do courses built on cases ensure that the celebrated ones do not subtly teach students that the press is right, no matter what procedures are used? Does our use of journalism cases really teach students how to fish or does it simply give them fish instead? Does this approach (at least when it predominates) enable students to reach justified moral judgments successfully?

If a minimal definition of ethics instruction means a vigorous and disciplined effort to analyze and solve vexing moral dilemmas, some distance remains yet to travel. That conclusion is not as judgmental as it sounds. Any area of investigation goes through several stages of intellectual evolution, and media ethics—teaching, research, and theory—is still at the beginning levels. It seems obvious that journalism ethics will not put down healthy roots without continuing and vigorous attention. Many of the problematics will only be resolved through ongoing experimentation and scholarly investigation.

4. The emerging basic pedagogical debate concerns whether ethics should be taught as a specific course or by absorbing ethics into courses throughout the curriculum.[20] This difference in educational philosophy is worthy of continued discussion. Further evaluation and research are needed to help determine the pedagogical efficacy of these two approaches before we can begin outlining the ideal program of ethics instruction. The saturate-the-curriculum option seems more natural, more nearly to emulate the situational, inductive necessities impinging on professionals throughout their careers. However, given the soft spots that appear at virtually all levels of the survey, one wonders whether the claim to teach ethics throughout the curriculum sometimes results from ignorance about ethics as a liberal arts discipline. If so, its treatment could be in very functional, ad hoc terms.[21] On the other hand, schools that include a specific course find that discussion of ethical issues at appropriate places elsewhere in the curriculum is much more likely and typically more intelligent as well. As a minimum, those who assert that ethical issues must be considered throughout the program should be pressed with the following questions: Is everyone just assuming ethical matters are

being treated, or is the faculty certain; who covers the issues and how; what normative framework is presented; are students forced to explain why they hold particular points of view? A concerted and systematic effort appears essential for sensitizing students and making their discussion of ethical problems in non-ethics courses more informed. The complexity of modern ethical dilemmas would seem to require a specific course in the curriculum. That conclusion filters through the data even though 73 percent of the respondents feel a special course is unnecessary.

While local particulars obviously vary, teaching such a course successfully demands instructors with appropriate qualifications. If the teacher has not specialized in academic ethics, he or she should at least be a "competent amateur" in this area.[22] That competency can be most directly ensured by a minimum of one year of course work in ethics, but other ways of gaining mastery of the subject matter are possible also. Continuing education for those teaching media ethics and membership in organizations such as the "Society for the Study of Professional Ethics" will provide helpful advance too. Team-teaching and supplementing the class with presentations by professionals and by ethicists can overcome instructor deficiencies to some extent also.

5. Those committed to a specific course in ethics (27 percent) fundamentally disagree over the location of that course in the curriculum. Three place this course in the philosophy department and two team-teach it (using an ethicist and a journalist). The other 59 (92 percent) offer it within the communications curriculum. In this latter category, one school uses an instructor with a Ph.D. in philosophy and the course therefore reflects a principial orientation to ethics as an academic enterprise. Nearly all of them, however—even though they have a course devoted solely to ethics—tend to treat the subject matter inductively as do the schools without such courses. The small number of courses geared directly to philosophical ethics exhibit a rather clear sense of direction and have a discernible conceptual framework. As with the noncourse option described above, more investigation is needed as to whether an ethics course outside the journalism program raises ethical awareness among students more than does a course directly within the journalism curriculum. An outside

course in its natural habitat might avoid simplistic personal moralism and articulate a more sophisticated social ethics. Reducing ethics to professional rectitude is always a greater danger when ethics is taught within the journalism department rather than outside it. One university explained the problem and its solution this way:

> We came to the realization that we were treating ethics strictly through a journalistic lens; we were looking at issues chiefly as journalists rather than primarily as members of society. We believe that journalists should be made more aware of problems of ethics from the viewpoints of society generally rather than journalism specifically. We approached the Philosophy Dept. They agreed to set up a course for us. The course has proved successful. It is now required for all journalism majors.

In this area, as in the preceding conclusion, the inside-the-curriculum option appears to have the larger numbers, but the outside-the-curriculum alternative a slightly better case.[23]

6. Law is involved as a major context for 30 percent of the courses. Moreover, of the instructors with at least some formal training (44 percent), nearly all have their training in law. "My credentials," wrote one respondent, "is that I am an attorney; I passed the ethics test of the California bar." Such factors indicate a need for discussion over the boundaries between ethics and law. No one in the survey views law as the maximum standard, and 48 respondents (75 percent) see it as only one element in determining ethics. In addition, four schools offer separate courses in both ethics and law, and most programs include a course in law by itself. No evidence emerged that any instructor completely reduced the moral to the legal. However, very few respondents consciously distinguished law and ethics as two different frames of reference. Once again, it merits further research whether courses combining the two do not influence students toward equating the legal with the ethical. Max Lerner notes in a wider study of the professions that a "bottom line" ethics typically emerges where minimum attention is paid to minimum standards in order to prevent personal catastrophe.[24]

The overall trend in the conceptualization of the issues among journalism educators seems biased toward legalization. This tends to make a crucial dimension (that is, the legal) virtually exclusive. It thereby confuses the philosophical distinction between the necessary and the sufficient; that is, rather than viewing the law as one necessary component in the analysis of issues, the legal dimension is often expanded to become a sufficient criterion for understanding them. The practical problems in maintaining two separate courses, however, are admittedly severe. As one respondent wrote:

> While it would be great to have courses both in press law and ethics, that option seems unlikely. We require three courses in reporting and newswriting, one in editing, one in photography, one in theory, one in press history, one in current issues, and one in law and ethics. This leaves journalism majors only two options among about ten electives to fill out the thirty-three semester hours required of majors. If we require a separate course in media ethics, we would have to cut something out of our program, and it is not clear what that would be.

III. Substantive Issues in Media Ethics Courses

Though there is little agreement about the formal place and purpose of ethics courses in journalism education, some consensus exists over content. A few common themes appear in nearly all the texts and courses. In order to place that conclusion in context and to ask what issues warrant emphasis in responsible ethics instruction, the present situation needs further description.

A. Content of Courses in Journalism Ethics

As noted above, 66 media ethics courses were taught in the spring of 1977.[25] The list of topics included here does not measure the relative weight given each one. Typically, instructors spend one week per subject, but the total number of areas covered in a semester or quarter varies from eight to twenty, with subsequent variation in the depth with which individual topics are treated.

1. Thirty percent of these courses (20) combine ethics and law. In those cases, the content is rather predictable, usually following the organization of the text (primarily Francois's *Mass Media Law and Regulation,* Gillmor-Barron's *Mass Communication Law,* or Nelson-Teeter's *Law of Mass Communication).* This course outline is typical:

    a. First Amendment Theory
    b. Prior Restraint of the Press
    c. Libel
    d. Privacy
    e. Constitutional and Statutory Rights in Newsgathering
    f. Confidential Sources
    g. Free Press vs. Fair Trial
    h. The Federal Communications Code
    i. Copyright and Plagiarism
    j. Obscenity, Pornography, and Censorship

2. It is very difficult to generalize about the content of those media ethics courses without a legal emphasis (62 percent). What follows are a few fairly broad subject areas which provide at least some clarification of the subject matter:

    a. Six common themes appear in nearly all 41 courses:

       i) *Problems on Daily Newsgathering.* Lapses that occur in regular gatekeeping chores. Handling of errors. Happy news. Dubious information-gathering methods. The recurring question is whether the press must give the audience what they are perceived to want or ought to have.

       ii) *Reporters and Sources.* Is the confidentiality privilege absolute or qualified? Under what conditions can newsmen justifiably suppress information? Even in criminal court proceedings? Problem of anonymous sources and leaks. Status of shield laws.

       iii) *Invasion of Privacy.* Legitimate public interest or merely titillating gossip, e.g., Capitol Hill sex scandals. Purloined documents. Defamation of public officials.

       iv) *Economic Temptations.* Payola. Freebies. Junkets.

       v) *National Security and Government Secrecy.* How do these civil necessities impinge on press freedom? Does the government, as Arthur Sylvester has suggested, have the right to lie under emergency circumstances? Freedom of Information Act.

       vi) *Efforts Toward Greater Responsibility.* The Codes of Ethics, for example, their content and purpose. Press Councils (national and local). Journalism Reviews. Right of reply (Op-Ed pages included). More professional behavior. Ombudsmen. Do alternative presses and styles of journalism provide better newsgathering?

b. Fifty percent of these courses include one or more themes in addition to the six core issues above:

vii) *Terror and Violence in News.* What is responsible coverage of civil disorder? What if violence is real, but contrived, as in terrorist attacks and kidnappings? Police and crime news. The press thrives on bad news; would such events occur less often if ignored?

viii) *Photojournalism.* Ethics of news photography. Sensationalism. Tastelessness. Should executions be shown or police in open combat with suspected criminals? NBC's gruesome TET film. Retouched, feigned, staged, manipulated photography. Composographs.

ix) *Bias.* Objectivity, or is Agnew correct? Proactivist, liberal, big city, prolabor bias?

x) *Institutional Pressures.* Internal pressure from management, advertisers, corporate profit, audience/subscription needs. External hazards: commercial promotions, government releases, advertising disguised as news. Media concentration limiting diversity of media voices.

xi) *Free Press/Fair Trial.* Some attention to strictly legal matters, but usually more concern with specific problems such as gag orders, cameras in the courtroom, Patty Hearst, Sam Sheppard, releasing information on juvenile offenders.

c. A few courses include one or more of these issues

xii) *Minorities.* Coverage of ethnic groups (blacks, American Indians, Latinos, etc.). Sex stereotypes. Racial demands (Black Panthers). Rivers-Schramm have a chapter in this area; the five courses using this text, plus one other course, include this topic.

xiii) *Fairness.* Equal access, balance, opposing views. Should newspapers bind themselves to the same guidelines as broadcasting?

xiv) *Deception and Falsehood.* Only three courses include this as a separate heading, though several include pseudo-events and deception in their treatment of daily newsgathering and photojournalism.

xv) *Sensationalism*. Three courses include this as a specific subject area rather than include it under photojournalism, violent news, or privacy invasion.

xvi) *Checkbook Journalism*. Two courses include this topic, though a few others mention it under daily newsgathering, and one course includes a case study of Robert Haldeman selling interviews.

d. Media ethics courses outside the journalism program confront, in varying detail, issues not included above: Are moral judgments objective or subjective? The journalist's responsibility for consequences. The perplexities of contentious actions. Assumptions underlying the new journalism and old. The ethics of democratic debate. Using evidence in advocacy. Changing the values in other cultures and subcultures.

These courses also tend to be more thematic in approach, emphasizing problems occurring more broadly within the humanities: credibility; truth-telling; respect for persons; utilitarianism; conflicts of interest; individualism; competitiveness.

B. Issues Shared With Professional Education Generally

Although the nuances and intellectual framework differ to some degree, journalism shares with the other professions the three issues discussed in *Ethics Teaching in Higher Education:* privacy and confidentiality, paternalism, whistle-blowing.[26] Introducing students to the important aspects of these issues is a desirable objective in all media ethics courses; however, given the nature of the journalism profession, privacy and confidentiality, along with truth-telling, merit the greatest attention. Paternalism and whistle-blowing need more scholarly attention outside the journalism classroom before they will prove to be usefully transferable concepts within it.

1. Community

One issue is the press's obligation to maintain a vital community life. Robert Park early asserted as a purpose of the metropolitan press a creation of the sense of community which had been lost to those who had moved from small towns to the big cities. However, the growth of the attitude of detached objectivity and its reflection in newspaper pages in the last half century has seemed to move in the opposite direction.[27]

"Readers feel strongly that newspaper staffs have no genuine sense of community," according to Arnold Rosenfeld, editor of the *Dayton* (Ohio) *News* and a perceptive observer of the press on the national scene. What people like least is the profession's prized ability to transmit facts without bias or feeling. "We desperately protest our good intentions. But the public doesn't understand, perhaps because we are not allowed by the rules to consider the consequences of publication—which is, I agree, our most important ethic—or its impact on the reader." A study recently completed for the American Society of Newspaper Editors has found that readers expect newspapers to be "more attentive to their personal needs, more caring, more warmly human." They want stories told in terms of "human feelings and compassion."[28] Such a concern is often "ignored in the macho world of daily journalism," says press critic Charles Seib of the *Washington Post*. "A common newsroom disease is petrification of the sense of common humanity."

The notion of private and public life stands at the center of journalistic structure and performance. The newsman's major appeal is the "public's right to know." Some of the media's most agonizing ethical problems arise specifically from the public/private nexus—reporting the personal lives of public officials, for example, the confidentiality of sources, and the government's right to secrecy for ensuring public safety.[29] Nearly all media ethics courses properly include a section on such topics. But only with a clear understanding of the community concept, and only with a strong commitment to fostering it, can important gains be achieved on these matters.

Historically, two of the greatest minds who focused on American democracy, Alexis de Tocqueville and John Dewey, both centered their analysis on this matter of public life. Tocqueville worried correctly that overzealous egalitarianism would finally leave only a naked state as the bulwark against social dissolution. John Dewey defined democracy as a mosaic of publics, and showed concern about these local face-to-face communities disappearing into a more abstract massified whole. It becomes clear that Tocqueville and Dewey—though separated by nearly a century, writing from different orientations, and focusing on different dimensions—highlight the same issue. It can also be noted that Walter Lippmann concentrated on this matter in his two significant books, *Public Opinion* and *The Public Philosophy*. In addition, Jacques Ellul pushes our thinking here even further. His perspective has some limitations, but Ellul does argue rather cogently that expansive media systems, under the guise of providing popular discussion, actually destroy public life by "gradually and imperceptibly" producing social conformity and political inebriation. Together these authors have identified an enduring intellectual problem which needs continued attention as a foundation for discussing the details of how journalists can treat national security information and the personal lives of public officials and their sources ethically.

2. Truthfulness

The journalist's obligation to truth is a standard part of the rhetoric. The Hutchins Commission in 1947 mentioned it, as do virtually all the codes. In fact, those in information instinctively recognize that the credibility of words is somehow central to the communication enterprise. Communicators tend to agree, at least in a low-level sense, with Karl Jaspers: "The moment of communication," he said, "is at one and the same time the preservation of, and a search for, the truth."[30]

However, except for a focus on the obligation to accuracy in reporting, ethics courses are very slight on truthfulness and its antonym, deception. Though they may treat them informally here and there, only three courses include deception as a separate heading. Media ethics instruction tends to be case-oriented rather than theme-oriented, but even allowing for that still leaves small evidence that journalism is morally perspicacious in this area. In the same curious sense that advertising scholars have given us little enlightenment on the nature of persuasion, so news people have not developed truthfulness as fully as its centrality would suggest. If one instructional goal is helping students recognize ethical issues, journalism faces a mountain of work here.

It seems reasonable to agree with Sissela Bok that "when regard for truth is even slightly weakened, all things become doubtful," and to consent to her thesis that an absolutely rigid rejection of all lies without any conditions seems untenable on various crisis occasions.[31] Therefore, what becomes important for the agenda in media ethics is massive assistance in finding such exceptions and thereby establishing valid boundaries. Perhaps a bottom line test case or two can be located where deception is morally permissible in journalism at crucial junctures. It is apparent, however, at this stage, that an ideology that continually stresses the rights and privileges of the press can easily permit all manner of deception without even the faintest hint of any moral dilemmas. Sissela Bok's suggestion, therefore, is an important one for journalism education, that is, tilting the relevant subject matter toward the principle of veracity, toward Aristotle's assumption that lies are mean and culpable.

Truthfulness also warrants careful attention because accuracy has been a constituent element in any basic definition of truthfulness. Someone once defined journalism as history in a hurry, and providing an accurate, representative account rarely occurs under those conditions. Unfortunately, getting the story first is now often rewarded more than getting it right. There are extraordinary pressures here, such as those Edward Jay Epstein describes. Journalism has few formal mechanisms for having others check the accuracy of newsgathering. Thus the search for truth and the enterprise of journalism are not synonymous.[32] Communication scholars can profitably participate in the wider debate over the nature of truth, and in the process can strengthen the understanding of truthfulness in journalistic practice.

3. Paternalism

Journalism does not confront this problem as directly as does law and medicine since it has no individually identifiable clients. If an obvious kind of paternalism is claiming superior knowledge and intervening on that basis in a client's circumstances without full consent, then journalists do not practice paternalism. Unlike government officials, they do not typically impose constraints on individual liberty in the name of promoting a person's own good.

However, editors and reporters easily become guilty of weak

forms of paternalism, of a patronizing benevolence. Their superior professional knowledge, firsthand experience with the situation being reported, and lofty intentions can lead them to demean the public. They stand in unequal relationship to their audience and readership, and work within an institutional form which often claims to be a major arbiter of knowledge and political insight.[33] In the same way that doctors and lawyers and social workers are paternalistic, if they do not give their clients control over decisions made in their behalf, so a nonpaternalistic journalism would provide information without implying that only one conclusion from these data is reasonable. Warnings against patronizing attitudes will be appropriate throughout the course, especially in the inevitable debates about giving the members of the public what they want or what they ''should have.'' Paternalism could provide a stimulating session or two in the editing and reporting courses as well.

4. Whistle-blowing

Most journalists are employees, frequently of enormous corporations in which money often plays the determinative role. Therefore, they must confront the same responsibilites for immorality within the organization as other workers in business, government, and medicine. They have an expanding circle of obligations as do employees generally. Making such duties clear in a media ethics course will be extraordinarily difficult, however. Journalists on the whole engage in very little mutual criticism, and instances of whistle-blowing are virtually nonexistent. The *Columbia Journalism Review* gives darts in each issue for questionable performances. The National and Minnesota News Councils, along with the few local press councils that exist, review criticisms of the media and make their investigations public. Nearly two dozen of the 1,700 daily newspapers have ombudsmen who monitor performance and publicly attack when necessary. However, generally speaking, whistle-blowing does not come naturally for journalists.

Another factor contributing to a reluctance to blow whistles may be the predominance of authoritarian rather than consensual patterns of decisionmaking implicit in the structure of the modern media corporation and extending into the newsroom. There is a low premium on challenge to authority, despite the newsman's pride in his "autonomy," and as a result, little encouragement, perhaps, to examine or act on one's own ethical priorities. The balancing process between personal and organizational values must be undertaken independently by journalists employed in these corporations, but they usually receive little organized encouragement from their superiors to do so. The good reporter's reaction to the fire alarm may be equated with his desired response to corporate authority—brisk and unquestioning.[34]

An aspect of the problem that merits further consideration in the classroom and beyond it is the media's role in deciding whether or not to publicize whistle-blowing by others, and thus to become participants in the act. Especially when whistle-blowers wish to remain anonymous and when their outrage may be petty or ill-focused, journalists who print their allegations risk furthering the goals of those who are unethical or disloyal. Some case studies that distinguish tattletales from whistle-blowers should be prepared so that reporters learn to discriminate between participation in responsible and irresponsible exposés.

C. Issues Resulting From Historical Circumstance

Two issues—codes and the adversary relationship—are important for media ethics courses to explore because of the particular history of journalism education and the journalism profession. The first is typically covered in courses now, though not always as deeply or carefully as it requires. The second is only rarely viewed as a moral problem.

1. Codes

Ethics courses should include a major address to the nature of codified morality since codes themselves play such an ambiguous role within journalistic practice. The meanings read into that set of symbols we call "codes," differ radically now from their time of origin. They may indeed have encouraged respectability in the 1920s when they were first drawn up. They helped to sanction those engaged in a vital social function. But today they often become parochial instruments for protecting tangible interests and preventing regulation. As outside attack on the media's power increases, as the curve of criticism rises, attackers expect more of an answer than an appeal to codes. In fact, if the press when criticized responds, in effect, that it has adopted a code and therefore is responsible, most critics are unimpressed. Students must be introduced to the reality of such altered circumstances and not simply indoctrinated into the codes' content.

Certainly codes can be presented as basic to daily habits. They serve as self-discipline devices. They do guide etiquette and therefore have some usefulness in today's situation. They have functional desirability. The Society of Professional Journalists and the *Columbia Journalism Review* and *Nieman Reports* and the National News Council have correctly urged that journalists adhere to them. Media courses which introduce students to codes should continue to include them. While leaving little space for ethical reflection, they do foster a morality of competence and help prevent highly offensive practices and materials.

Instructors grant too much, however, if they do not go beyond codes themselves to the broader problem of accountability and the rites of passage into the profession. Codes will continue to play some role in journalism since membership in any profession by definition entails not just success but integrity. Courses need to overcome the instrumental ways codes are often treated and to grapple with the students over the very nature of professional structures. Codes thus can serve as an entree for treating the broader issue of professionalization itself. Some basis for vocational independence is essential; if enforceable codes do not serve appropriately for journalism, perhaps a different, more preferable professional structure can take shape from these discussions.[35]

2. Adversarity

The adversary relationship stands at the heart of newsgathering. Since Thomas Jefferson, journalists have perceived themselves as vigilant watchdogs. Students thus are socialized into what is usually a healthy skepticism about government officials. In extreme cases, one hears these slogans in journalism classrooms and newsrooms: "Our enemy, the government"; "All politicans are liars"; "When looking at officials, look down on them."[36]

Adversarity needs attention as a substantive issue in a media ethics course, though perhaps time constraints will limit that attention to one or two classes. The adversary notion in the post-Watergate era may have come to overdefine the nature of press-government relations.[37] Instructors may concede too much if they uncritically begin with adversariness as a cornerstone of journalistic philosophy. Certainly, Jefferson intended that the very premises of the social system be challenged; but if such embattlement is crucial for adequate reporting at all, how can that be limited to confrontations with government? Why should all social institutions not be included? Is the adversary relationship really essential for maintaining independence? Further, are fairness and dispassionate observation—also important journalistic values— compatible with the adversary notion?

But obviously the main concern in media ethics courses should be the justification or rejection of adversariness from an ethical perspective. It certainly seems morally problematic, for example, from the viewpoint of a teleological ethics where man is treated as an end. And on the practical level, in the process of inculcating adversarity, instructors might appear to encourage deception. Press-government cronyism destroys media effectiveness, to be sure. Yet James Thomson rightly pleads for compassion in the journalist's style.[38] Moral philosophy can help analyze adversariness sufficiently so that a more humanistic journalism emerges which is morally unimpeachable and yet provides the persistence, toughness, and assertive posture that journalism needs to disseminate information competently.

D. Implications

In many undergraduate courses it will be difficult to deal with more than eight to ten substantive issues, and there is little reason not to include the six items outlined above in 2–a: problems of daily newsgathering, reporters and sources, invasion of privacy, economic temptations, national security and government secrecy, codes of ethics. The issue meriting considerably greater coverage is deception and falsehood; some courses presently introduce that subject by including Sissela Bok's *Lying: Moral Choice in Public and Private Life* as a required text.

Upper-level seminars undoubtedly provide a better opportunity to confront—at least in limited fashion—paternalism, whistle-blowing, adversariness, and several other issues listed under 2–b and 2–c above. Such problems might also be covered by having the instructor in media ethics teach some sessions in the reporting and editing classes.

In any case, this is a heavy agenda and suggests the importance of a separate course which can encourage students to confront these matters by balancing the large view with attention to their immediate job demands and responsibilities. In a formal way, a specific course can bring the insights of liberal education to bear on prospective professional problems. It can focus on the tripartite nature of the journalist's moral and legal responsibilities—to self, to organization, to the public at large. Because of this important capstone quality, a course devoted solely to ethics or to ethical decisionmaking, within a context also emphasizing social responsibility, should be a required part of every journalism curriculum immediately preceding the awarding of the degree—undergraduate or graduate.

Important steps have already been taken toward this end. A new emphasis on courses specifically devoted to ethics (as opposed to those with more traditional concerns for "social responsibility") has now been written into accreditation standards for the American Council for Education in Journalism, the national accrediting body. Accredited schools are now specifically required to focus on education in ethics, and to monitor the quality of the ethical instruction given in other courses through the curriculum. Up to this time, the ACEJ has shown a disinclination to require specific courses in any area, considering such a direct demand as infringement on academic freedom. But the new emphasis on ethics as a mandated area of concern is an important step toward moving it from its present fringe position in many curricula.

IV. Instructional Objectives

It seems desirable that journalism schools endorse the five instructional goals which are identified and specified in the Report of the Hastings Center Project on *The Teaching of Ethics in Higher Education*.[39] They are: (1) stimulating the moral imagination; (2) recognizing moral issues; (3) developing analytical skills; (4) eliciting a sense of moral obligation and personal responsibility; and (5) tolerating—and resisting—disagreement and ambiguity. However, while agreeing that all five goals are essential for an adequate media ethics course, goal five needs little further comment. Two of the remaining four are especially adaptable to journalism education, whereas the other two are extraordinarily difficult to achieve.

Goal five of the Report (tolerating—and resisting—disagreement and ambiguity) needs attention as does the statement in the Report concerning the ability to dispense with the need for the teacher. But mentioning these two matters seems sufficient. There is virtually no evidence that journalism classrooms are mindlessly promoting ideological ethics and undisputed conventions. On the whole, journalism educators understand the necessity of making themselves dispensable. The strong professional influence on academic life, in fact, gives most instructors an insecure sense that they are not indispensable at all. Incompetent educators and poor courses do violate these goals at times, but few would dispute that they are worthy pursuits.

A. Recognizing Ethical Issues

The first of the major instructional goals set out in the Report that is compatible with journalism education generally is recognizing ethical issues. Engaging students in assessment and the use of cognitive judgment are both prized in the curriculum. Thus, when media ethics courses aim toward appraisal and teach students to examine ethical concepts and principles, other instructors agree with those objectives and recognize their validity.

The Socratic method is an eminently desirable way of enabling students to recognize ethical issues. This approach has been demonstrated at several media conventions and journalism conferences by Arthur R. Miller of the Harvard Law School. Richard Schwarzlose has also developed many practical suggestions for using this technique in university classrooms.[40] By means of Socratic sessions students can provide each other with ethically acceptable reactions to journalism problems and sharpen one another's ability to discover the ethical dimensions of various practices and policies. While becoming aware of their own ignorance on various topics, if guided effectively, students become much more precise in their definitions of concepts and principles.

The Socratic method is particularly useful for two kinds of ethical cases—those news situations charged with emotion and violence, and those involving ethically insoluble news problems. The first category embraces coverage of murder, suicide, marriage quarrels, drugs, illegitimate children, and so on, where hearsay, gossip, confession, and prior police records are the typical information sources. The second category includes covering a candidate for public office with a shady background, a prominent right-to-lifer concealing an abortion, transcripts of wiretaps which give secret information about government policy that contradicts public statements. "Each journalism class is a goldmine of uncertain and vacillating responses to journalistic problems. Socratic method mines and hauls to the surface this rich vein for all to see and think about."[41]

B. Developing Analytical Skills

Another of the goals of the Report that fits well with journalism education is developing analytical skills. As in other aspects of media study, ethical concepts are often disputed and logical skills can aid in achieving coherence and consistency. The mass media profession demands powerful skills for interpreting very complex events. Therefore, analytical abilities are sought to varying degrees in all media courses.

Achieving this goal demands that students apply and extend course material effectively. Lectures, notes, and examinations do not seem ideally designed for achieving this goal. The decision-making process must be placed at the center instead. Rather than simply introducing topics and readings, sending students through an explicit series of decisionmaking steps will increase the likelihood of successful problem-solving rather than leaving this proficiency to happy chance.

Instructors must demonstrate in the classroom that reaching adequate conclusions is a painstaking matter, with each of the problem areas organized around a series of explicit procedures.[42] If a teacher attempts to lead students in an unstructured discussion, the decisionmaking process is usually too sophisticated, confusing, or trial-and-error prone to have any value as model. Ideally, learning is a slow-motion experience in problem-solving and demonstrates attention to evidence, to valid argument, to patience with complexities.

The following steps can illustrate one way for the problem-solving framework to operate in developing analytical skills.

Step One: Have students identify the problem or issue at stake and state precisely why it is problematical at all. Getting the problem focused (or, as it might be called, "formulating a well-conceived hypothesis") is incredibly difficult. If the adversary notion is considered an ethical issue, for example, in what sense is that true? What precisely is morally objectionable about it? Does not some counterevidence seem to indicate that the press is actually too cozy with government?

Step Two: Students should generate possible solutions. They should offer all options, large and small, which come to mind for resolving the problem. Brainstorming techniques help cover this phase adequately. Students can be encouraged to present all suggestions in rapid succession regardless of how ridiculous they may seem. Finally, duplicates can be eliminated and suggestions grouped according to various themes.

Step Three: Students should choose a resolution and include as much information as relevant to explicate their choice. Full description would include, as a minimum, an identification of the hypotheses, unstated assumptions, and main ideas.

Step Four: The approach selected should be evaluated in terms of its substance, thoughtfulness, and feasibility. Somewhere in the defense, students should show how and why (or why not) the solution fits within the major ethical positions developed throughout history. The solution must also respond to the relevant objections that can be leveled against it. Evidence should also be forthcoming that matters of cost, personnel, and organizational realities have been considered.

Pertinent cases usually assist in steps one and two. Careful attention to each phase promotes well-conceived approaches. And while eliminating superficiality, using the educational process to generate responsible conclusions helps prevent an iconoclasm which never contributes anything constructive.

C. Stimulating the Moral Imagination

Another goal of media ethics instruction—stimulating the moral imagination—does not correspond well to typical journalism practice and instruction. For students to understand that the moral point of view is basic, their emotional side must be evoked. A focus on empathy and caring indicates that a journalism ethics course is more than an abstract intellectual exercise.

However, as a minimum, the moral imagination will not be stimulated until live human beings and their welfare become central. That concern stands far distant from journalism at present. The journalist is subjected to peculiar demands stemming from the "clients" for his professional services. As noted earlier, "client" may actually be an inappropriate word; there is no single individual or set of individuals with identifiable demands, vulnerabilities, and needs. Journalists only see a vast, undifferentiated "general public" looming amorphous on the horizon. They have a frustrating sense of shooting arrows off into oblivion. Idealists are sustained by a conviction akin to that of the public servant—that they are indeed serving a public good, that the public has a right to the information they provide. But there is almost no evidence of direct impact, and little feeling of working for individual human beings.

Nonetheless, to serve this vast, general audience, the journalist must develop a set of detached intellectual skills. Confronted with complexity he must be able to identify what he believes to be its core, and then compose an account presenting that essence with force and clarity in terms understandable to the largest number and variety of people. "The ability to simplify clutter into large comprehensible, apprehensible shapes" has been identified by Kenneth Clark as the consummate quality of the artist.[43] Scientists and statesmen also must reduce the complex to the simple. In their extraction of the essence of day-to-day events, journalists share in that undertaking. But they must react and reduce with speed and assurance. There is less premium on the conditional or speculative state of mind; the need for intellectual closure comes with every new deadline.

Perhaps it is this constant necessity to impose closure; perhaps it is the journalist's basic conviction that it is not his responsibility but that of the public's to impose meaning and deal with consequences. Whatever the shaping forces, the journalist tends to deal very little with the consequences of his reportage. He tends to assume that publication is the ultimate responsibility. He provides the "facts"; once they are published, it is assumed that an abundance of ideas competing in the marketplace will make all come out right. The concept has sturdy philosophic roots beginning with the *Areopagitica*. A combination of such historical justification, perhaps, with contemporary publishing pressures tends to render the journalist less sensitive to the consequences of his publishing, particularly the impact on individual source, subject, or member of the audience. Rights of the individual are usually considered within a legal framework prescribing rights of privacy, fair trial, or preservation of reputation. Ethical responsibilities aside from those required by law tend less often to come under critical scrutiny. More recent codes of ethics—such as that of the Society of Professional Journalists—admonish journalists to show respect for the "dignity, privacy, rights and well-being of people in the course of gathering and presenting the news." But even in this statement, only two of the news media's three functions (gathering and preparing) are considered. The third part of the process of communication (dissemination) and the effects of such dissemination on individual human beings, as separate and identifiable parts of the mass, tend frequently to be ignored.[44]

A lively sense of the moral relationship between prospective journalists and the people they will encounter in the future can be elicited in a variety of ways. What is necessary is not only an experience of intellectual encounter with the issues, but the envisioning of a series of situations in which future ethical dilemmas will be played out. What can be created is a kind of Altamira cave of the imagination, something like those real prehistoric caves where Jacob Bronowski suggests young hunters may have used the power of anticipation to face the idea of dangers to come. "When the hunter was brought here into the secret dark and the light was suddenly flashed on the pictures, he saw the bison as he would have to face him, he saw the running deer....The moment of fear was made present to him....an experience which he would have and which he needed not to be afraid of."[45]

This "forward-looking imagination" can be cultivated by encounters, not only with practicing journalists brought to the classroom, but with people whose lives have been affected by journalists—a scientist, perhaps, who had his work more or less conscientiously and accurately presented, or a businessman dreading to wake every morning to the day's ration of doom and terror in the news. Role playing is the next step, involving the students imaginatively in demanding situations. Actual historic quandaries—the encounter at the upper echelons of the *New York Times* which debated the suppression of news of the Bay of Pigs, for example—can be played out with a variety of possible ends devised and moral positions evoked. Judicious use of news photos is valuable also.

Probably the most effective in eliciting a sense of sympathetic introspection is the film. Hollywood has made 1,700 films on people in the media in the past fifty years; a number of them focus directly on moral conflict. *Network* is a prime example of ethical clash between those devoted to profit and those to valid news; *Big Carnival* focuses on the newsman's obligations to truth-telling; *Gentleman's Agreement* on the dangers of bias. The list is endless; characters and situations evoke the complexity of actual decisionmaking in a way that lectures and case study and unadorned discussion can rarely parallel.[46]

D. Eliciting Moral Obligation

The fourth goal of the Report, eliciting a sense of moral obligation and personal responsibility, is likewise difficult within contemporary journalism education. Ethics instruction must properly appeal to the will, expect action, and engage volition. For all practical purposes, it is presupposed that individuals are free to make moral choices and be held responsible for them. But two situations in the journalism profession impinge on this freedom and make the implementation of this goal very problematical.

First is the temporal dimension mentioned above. Pressured to speed of action by fear of competition and by highly accelerated technology, journalists live in an atmosphere of urgency. They must make important decisions against impending deadlines. Action is important, not refusal to act for whatever consideration of consequence. Again the rhetoric is instructive. There is the rule of thumb, "refusal to publish cannot be justified on the basis of foreseeable harm." The century-old tag, "publish and be damned," is no longer acknowledged by thoughtful modern news executives, but its spirit still seems to hang in city-room air.

The temporal dimension also affects the journalist's treatment of the reality to be reported. There is little time for contemplation or interpretation in the usual news day. Fittingly enough to these demands for speed, the day is divided into events, what the historian H. Stuart Hughes has called segments of the endless web of experience "torn out of context for purposes of clearer understanding."[47]

According to this classic concept, "news" arises naturally from events. The journalist is to be an objective, detached, neutral channel between events and reader.[48] He does not impose himself on the events. As colorless conduit, he feels a primary responsibility to the accuracy of report, validation of fact and speed of transit, trusting readers to ferret out many of the implications and meanings for themselves.[49] In case of conflict between speed of report and accuracy or completeness of report, there is an ethical tension. But the deadline looms; the decision must be made. The classic response has been to fall back on the older value. "Go with what you've got'' has been the traditional imperative.[50]

The peculiar episodic conception of the undertaking colors the professional mind-set and reward system. Deadlines are harsh, but rewards are immediate—a broadcast completed, a story published, the by-line in type or on the air. The day is over, the news put out, the psychic reward realized. Problems are resolved with each deadline or implicitly put off until the next chunk of day to be covered. This system of instant rewards and postponed problems actually becomes satisfying, shaping the journalist's mode of valuing and behaving. It is difficult to feel morally obligated for the complex after-effects which may result from the news account. Of necessity, present action is more important than preparation or consequence.[51]

A second constraint on freedom of decision, also noted briefly above, is the journalist's operation within the larger economic framework of a corporation for which the primary imperative is profit. Unlike lawyers or physicians, the journalist almost of necessity must exist within an organization whose chief executive officers often are not members of his own profession.

Financial priorities also serve to restrict resources necessary for interpretive, investigative, and analytic approaches to news, and for contemplation of their consequences. Economic pressures for rapid publication and for outdistancing any competition reinforce the values of routinized ''objective'' reporting and reduce time for considering the ethical implications of action. The lawyer may be easily within reach to consult on possible legal liability; but the bioethicist now available for consultation on ethical problems in some hospitals and laboratories has as yet no counterpart on the city desk.

Historically, the most compelling moral obligation has been phrased in negative terms—not to let anything interfere with publication of material considered worthy by institutionalized standards of news judgment. Pressures from government, business, special-interest groups, individuals, or the newsman's own publisher are to be resisted, according to the accepted ethic. This obligation seems to be the reason why conflict of interest assumes such a primary position in the traditional journalist's ethical code. Anything that interferes with a disinterested presentation of the news is a primary threat. A second negative obligation is the duty to ignore consequences of publication, mentioned above. The primary positive obligation is to the interests of the general public, envisioned as incorporating the body of voters who need data on which to base informed political choice.

In any event, open discussion of ethical, as separate from legal, issues is relatively rare in the newsroom or when groups of reporters or editors are gathered together. The more abstract discussions tend to halt with invocation of "First Amendment" or "right to know." Only a few professional organizations have committees on ethics specifically labeled as such.[52] Admission of doubt or guilt does not correspond with the newsman's tough and resilient self-image, and frequently appears self-destructive in the corporate game.

E. Summary

The traditional model in the profession, it has been argued, is the propensity to view life as a series of episodes rather than as a continuing stream of experience. Individuals react rapidly to situations on the basis of previously internalized standards of news judgment, focus on action rather than consequences, expect immediate gratification, come quickly to conclusions. These journalists have been conditioned to remain aloof from events, to suspend judgment, to act as disinterested observers rather than participants. There is a focus on the ad hoc response, and less on appeals to principle or theory as a framework for decisionmaking.

To the degree that journalism students are conditioned to the traditional model, approaches they are encouraged to develop will conflict with the educational goals outlined above. Thus a course in media ethics must be especially concerned to encourage in students the consideration of long-term consequences as well as immediate action, the tolerance of ambiguity and unresolved dilemmas, the slow and deliberate coming to judgment, the invocation of principle and sense of moral obligation. All these are qualities that the episodic view of the world and the neutral posture tend to devalue, and those teaching ethics must address themselves frequently and directly to this tension.

Certainly it is the goal of professional education to provide immediately usable skills and attitudes valuable in the newsroom.

But it is a companion purpose—perhaps best realizable in the ethics course—to preserve and protect those more humane considerations sometimes trampled in the rush to deadline. The prospective journalist should be conditioned to the more philosophic long-term view to balance the pressures toward the narrow and the episodic approach that will characterize the professional milieu.

Consideration of this conflict should influence method and substance in teaching ethics. As a method, case studies—now the most frequently used teaching tool—will continue to be valuable. These involve both the event and the narrative essential to the journalistic approach. Therefore, because of the form as well as substance, case studies are appropriate, as are contacts with working professionals and films. Consideration of theory, however, should bound consideration of specific problems, giving students some idea of the resources available through different theoretical approaches for resolving ethical quandaries, and some tolerance of the very state of the quandaries themselves.

Attention to ethical theories of consequences may also tend to counterbalance the typical professional focus on the act of publication itself as a sort of ultimate good. When journalists deliberately contemplate the consequences of their work, for the most part, it is only in terms of their significance within the political sphere. The impact of the media on government—the political environment and the public attitude toward government policy—has been a primary consideration and indeed rationale for journalism since its colonial origins. Thorough attention to consequentialist theory can emphasize more detailed consideration of the extra-political sphere, particularly the impact on individuals—sources, subjects, and the lives of individual readers. In fact, invoking responsible consequentialist approaches will help call attention to ethical questions involved not only in gathering and publishing news, but to that perhaps more neglected dimension among media ethicists to date—impact of *distribution* on individuals as well as on the body politic.[53]

Moreover, the course on ethics must address itself to the multiple responsibility of journalists, not only to the traditional concern for the public welfare and to journalists' personal sense of moral obligation, but the integrity of the corporation by which they are employed. As professional newspeople are sandwiched into a corporate structure whose executives are primarily concerned with profit, the news can easily become just another product to be stamped out as the market demands. The journalist bears some responsibility for ethical decisionmaking at the organizational as well as the personal level; in fact, in many situations the publisher is also the editor and therefore faces even more acutely the need to balance organizational survival and integrity. Courses in ethics must give students some guidance in bringing ethical insights to bear on conflicts between personal and organizational commitments. The responsibility to the public sphere must be borne by both individual and organization.

V. Major Intellectual Concern

Alongside the classroom work described so far, working out an applied ethics for journalism could well become the foremost scholarly objective and be the catalyst for further advance. Perhaps this only suggests a nomenclature for most journalism educators. Applied ethics is proposed here as distinct from descriptive ethics on the one side and metaethics on the other. Descriptive ethics reports on the actual moral behavior of given persons and groups. Metaethics is the philosophical study of ethical theories, the status of moral claims, and such questions as whether value judgments can be established or justified.[54]

In no sense should either be depreciated. But the challenge for journalism at present lies in applied ethics. In this approach one retains an interest in the making of concrete moral judgments, in the way ethical decisionmaking ought to function in the media professions. The concern for principle, for generality, that prompts the best metaethics is retained as well. Thus educators and professionals are of necessity pulled together in a mutual effort.

The two sides are not just mindlessly syncretized, but creatively fused. The search is for considered normative judgments, for principial statements about classes of conduct judged as right or wrong, for states of affairs and traits of character that can be praised or blamed. If descriptive ethics moves into the forefront and becomes the exclusive domain, it tends toward a relativistic ethics. If metaethics dominates, it becomes a self-contained circle, out of touch with reality.

Lest applied ethics as a primary intellectual pursuit sound too irrelevant, a historical footnote may be apropos. When faced in the 1920s with a moral skepticism and collapsing standards and institutional assault similar to the present decade, Walter Lippmann responded in 1929 with *A Preface to Morals*. Lippmann searched philosophy, theology, history, and sociology for a system of values strong and relevant to postwar conditions. His reconstruction, far from being considered bizarre, became a bestseller (six editions the first year) and a rallying point for a broadly based exploration that played an influential role in standing against the nihilism and despair usually associated with the twenties.

No one needs to defend any longer the truism that worthwhile casuistry depends on a principled framework, but perhaps another digression, this time to Aristotle, will make the point more precise. Aristotle established that moral knowledge is of a specific kind. Moral knowledge, in his work, is similar to technical skill, in that it must be applied concretely; and, while limiting the intellection of Socrates and Plato, Aristotle did not eradicate theoretical knowledge as an essential component of moral reflection either. Yet moral consciousness for Aristotle cannot be equated with *techne* nor with theoretics *(episteme);* thus he establishes ethics as a discipline independent of both art and metaphysics.[55] Likewise the appeal to applied ethics is a two-edged sword. Formulating ethics too much in terms of professional life inevitably means that the formulations become dominated by routine processes directed toward the technical ends served by that profession. Ethical statements then arise from what Whitehead called ''minds in a groove.'' But a system of abstract generality is not a substitute either. Applied ethics appeals to the moral consciousness, to man's interpretative capacity, and not solely to practice or to bare theorizing. One danger, incidentally, in the otherwise felicitous arrangement of team-teaching a media ethics course with a professional and a philosopher, is that both might emphasize their sides so much that the moral consciousness is not touched.

This is not the occasion for developing the concept of applied ethics with any kind of depth, though three selected themes suggest the dimensions and shape of a reasonable agenda.

First, mass communication scholars must produce an appropriate social ethics. Certainly, personal conscience and social morality should be treated as the proverbial two sides of the same coin, or as ethics in the narrow and broad sense. Where one begins and concentrates, however, greatly influences the overall construction. The seeds of this institutional sensitivity lie already in the press-government-society debates. The Hutchins Commission provided hints through its social responsibility theory, although hampering its vision by not making it intellectually sophisticated enough. An ethics born of social structures that is advocated here takes its inspiration from Alexis de Tocqueville, Emile Durkheim, T.S. Eliot, and Reinhold Niebuhr, and works from the contention that a society or community is more than a simple aggregation of its discrete elements.

A second theme—telos—is interwoven with the others, but receives so much attention in moral philosophy that it warrants separate consideration. An applied ethics needs to refine journalism's goals. One need not untangle all the complications surrounding "ends" since Aristotle to appreciate its general significance in any reflective ethical address.

The "public's right to know," in one sense, is an important democratic commitment; however, it is not an adequately developed goal for newsgathering and easily becomes an excuse for immoral behavior when gathering information. A more precise definition of the press's role—asked in terms of its responsibility as an institution to society as a whole—will aid in scaling down some of the press's imperialistic claims, giving it a crucial role in democratic life without making it both judge and administrator, spectator and actor.[56]

Third, as a minimum, applied ethics takes justifiability seriously. The principles and standards that emerge in a normative approach are those that are justified on grounds that others do not find defective. In judging press behavior—its publication of documents that were obtained deceptively, for example—that behavior, to be moral, must finally meet the test of acceptability by those not directly enfranchised.[57]

However, not only must normative standards arise through the justifying principle, but this operates diachronically also. Conclusions should take seriously the history of moral philosophy and bring this history to bear on the issues of journalism as a distinctive undertaking. Conclusions can be strengthened and idiosyncrasies erased if held before a tribunal of value theorists. Thus, if there are roots both in ethical systems and in public justification, the result is a system of moral obligations.

These are only formal statements. If once it is agreed that an applied ethics is an important pursuit, then the interesting debate about content can begin.

IV. Recommendations

While continuing to work on the more elusive and fundamental matters, there are several practical steps which can be taken to improve the teaching of journalism ethics. Several recommendations, in addition to those implied or suggested so far, seem obvious:

A. Overall Planning

1. Journalism needs the equivalent either of the "Commission on the Teaching of Bioethics" established by the Hastings Center, or the "Institute on Law and Ethics" sponsored by the Council for Philosophical Studies.[58] The recommendations will differ, but extended thinking by an interdisciplinary group can aid in shaping course content, curriculum organization, teaching formats, teacher training, and relationships with media practitioners.

B. Research

2. Research in Descriptive Ethics. Work in descriptive ethics must be stimulated. Several research projects have been recently completed or are presently under way which provide details about actual ethical behavior in the journalism profession. Sanders and Chang, for example, have investigated professional reaction to ethics codes.[59] Herbert Altschull has studied secrecy in the newsroom and the values used in printing or withholding informa-

tion.[60] Johnstone's ambitious study, mentioned earlier, illuminates the values held by American newspeople. Norman Van Tubergen and colleagues have initiated a series of studies based on the Q-methodology of the ethical behavior patterns of American reporters.[61] The McCormick Studies are accumulating representative cases of on-the-job professional behavior in ethical matters.[62] Todd Hunt has studied the role of ethics codes in New Jersey newspapers.[63] More such research projects must be designed, funded, and reported, including some which deal with the informal professional networks imposing sanctions for violation of ethical norms.

3. Research in Applied Ethics. Journalism education must participate in the larger enterprise of developing applied ethics with the professions as a whole. The improvement of media ethics instruction and the formulation of significant ethical statements for journalism will depend to a large extent on the broader development of practical, professional ethics. Journalism education needs to contribute literature and theory and research in all phases of this larger endeavor. A "Society and the Professions" program at Washington and Lee University takes this wider perspective seriously by offering studies, not only in journalism ethics, but in preprofessional law and medical ethics as well.

4. Interdisciplinary Research. Instructors should be encouraged toward interdisciplinary curriculum design, research, and writing on media ethics. Several universities provide such a program already, and in this case a moral philosopher and media scholar could profitably spend a summer or semester working in concert. Only three media ethics courses are now team-taught, and financial strictures may prevent that mode of instruction from blossoming. However, the design and research phases can be fruitfully carried out through a long-term partnership to accomplish the depth which more perfunctory interdisciplinary efforts cannot produce.

C. Teaching

5. Support for Teaching. Better communication networks can be built among those teaching media ethics. The equivalent of six

journals of medical ethics does not exist in journalism, but professional organizations and magazines and conventions provide an arena for exchanging outlines, recommending materials, debating curricula, and suggesting instructional techniques. It is especially important that the five courses with a philosophical bearing receive fuller description and more attention. Likewise, the present penchant for asserting that ethics is being satisfactorily taught when touched on throughout the curriculum must confront the realities of an enormous amount of complex subject matter. As such discussion goes on within the journalism fraternity, the necessary textbooks, reflective essays, and classroom materials will begin to emerge. Of great assistance in this exchange would be the openness of major journals such as the *Journalism Quarterly* to thoughtful essays on ethics. In fact, the time may not be too far distant when a separate newsletter on media ethics and even a specific journal on the subject will become necessary.

6. Liberal Environment for Teaching. An adequate journalism ethics cannot prosper in a professional school environment too largely saturated by trade-school assumptions emphasizing entry-level skills, or dominated by the fashionable focus on communication theory and research oriented primarily to the social sciences. The teaching of ethics can flourish only where educators cultivate the ability to recognize and distinguish between the problems that are moral and those that are scientific, and between those that are technological and those that are artistic. Such educators emphasize the significance of according each its appropriate sphere. They demonstrate the relationship of such distinctions to a valid professional life. Their students come to realize that living such a life places heavy demands on both imagination and intellect.

There is considerable continuing authority in journalism education to support its historic insistence on the liberal arts as the foundation for professional education. This continuing commitment to the humane values needs to be maintained, particularly in the face of demands for increased course work in the new technologies of both print and broadcast journalism. Medical education early succumbed to the lures of overwhelming emphasis on the physical sciences; only in recent decades have some medical schools increased the liberal components of student curricula. Journalism education (with its accrediting body continuing to demand that three-fourths of student course work be outside the professional curriculum, and to emphasize increasingly such liberal elements as media history and media ethics within that curriculum) may be able to avoid a similar cul-de-sac. To this end, those concerned with journalism ethics cannot merely work out the theoretical dimension in their ethics courses, but must address themselves to enriching the liberal component of the educational enterprise as a whole.

D. Relations With Practitioners

7. Cooperation With Practitioners. It is recommended that those interested in teaching and research in journalism ethics develop a pattern of cooperation with ethics committees of professional organizations. Several professional groups such as the American Society of Newspaper Editors, the National Conference of Editorial Writers, the Society of Professional Journalists/Sigma Delta Chi, and the Associated Press Managing Editors have committees specifically devoted to ethics or professional standards. Such professional societies typically also have more broadly titled committees on social responsiblity or freedom of information. Direct cooperation between these committees and the schools (perhaps through such a vehicle as the Committee on Professional Freedom and Responsibility of the Association for Education in Journalism) might clarify concerns of both groups and result in more effective education and practice.

8. Continuing Education For Practitioners. Spurred by the Nieman Fellows as the premiere example, journalism educators are increasingly recognizing the importance of continuing education. Media practitioners need opportunities for moral reflection as much as do any other professionals. The suggestions in section E. of the '' Institute on Law and Ethics Report'' (f.n. 48, pp. 25–27) are ideally suited for journalism, especially the week-long or weekend seminars focused on particular ethical problems. Because Nieman, the *Columbia Journalism Review,* SPJ/SDX, and

the National News Council are recognized for their contribution to professional ethics, they might cooperate with a university or two in playing host to a series of such seminars experimenting with different objectives and formats. State Humanities Councils are likely possibilities also as sponsors of two- to three-day working conferences which bring professionals and academics into discussion on various ethical problems.

Notes

1. See, for example, Jerome D. Frank, "Mental Health in a Fragmented Society—The Shattered Crystal Ball," *American Journal of Orthopsychiatry,* July 1979.

2. We are especially grateful for helpful criticisms of an earlier draft by James Boylan, Everette Dennis, Donald Gillmor, Russell Hurst, William Rivers, and Howard Ziff.

3. Cf. William R. Lindley, *Journalism and Higher Education: The Search for Academic Purposes,* (Stillwater, Okla: Journalistic Services Monograph).

4. Richard Hofstader, *The Progressive Movement 1900–1915* (Englewood Cliffs, N.J.: Prentice-Hall, 1963), pp. 1–15; also his *The Age of Reform* (New York: Random House, Vintage, 1955), pp. 4–59.

5. The word "professional" will be used throughout this monograph in the nontechnical sense as those forms of work that demand responsible performance and require formal training. Most media practitioners respond positively to this low-level definition in the sense that "acting like a professional" refers to better performance. As noted later, because the strong exclusivistic version of professionalism entails codes and controlling organizations, it has not taken root in journalism.

6. Frank W . Scott, "The Illinois Code," *Journalism Bulletin* 2, no. 2 (1925): 28.

7. E. M. Johnson, "The Utilization of the Social Sciences," *Journalism Bulletin* 4, no. 2 (1937): 30–35.

8. For a review of some historical aspects and an analysis of professionalization in contemporary journalism, see James W. Carey, "A Plea for The University Tradition: AEJ Presidential Address," *Journalism Quarterly* 55, no. 4 (Winter 1978): 846–55.

9. Walter Gieber, "The Attributes of a Reporter's Role," and Walter Gieber and Walter Johnson, "The City Hall 'Beat': A Study of Reporter and Source Roles," *Journalism Quarterly* 38 (Summer 1961): 289–97.

10. A recent discussion of historical influences on newsroom assumptions appears in Michael Schudson, *Discovering the News: A Social History of American Newspapers* (New York: Basic Books, 1978). The discussion here centers on the newspaper because of its formative influence on subsequent means of news transmission. Similar pressures and opportunities in radio and television newsrooms and in editorial offices of periodicals tend to be associated with similar ethical profiles.

11. A different viewpoint on this matter is presented by one of the respondents to an earlier draft of this paper: "In my experience, today's separation of the news and business departments in most newspapers tends to shield the reporter from the business aspects and lets him concentrate on the news-editorial functions."

12. Gaye Tuchman, "Making News By Doing Work: Routinizing the Unexpected," *American Journal of Sociology* 73 (July 1973): 111–31.

13. Early influential studies of newsroom socialization came from Warren Breed, "Social Control in the Newsroom," *Social Forces* 33 (May 1955): 326–35.

14. Cf. Michael Ryan, "Tough Question: To Judge or Not Judge the Media," *Journalism Educator* 34, no. 1 (April 1979): 3–5, 42.

15. Clifford G. Christians, "Variety of Approaches Used in Teaching Media Ethics," *Journalism Educator* 33, no. 1 (April 1978): 3–8, 24. A one-page form was mailed early in 1977 to heads of the 247 journalism and mass communication programs listed in the January 1977 *Journalism Educator*. Response was exceptional: 237 of the 247 questionnaires were returned (96 percent), with 100 percent response from the 67 accredited sequences in the list. This first survey identified 66 schools with specific courses devoted to ethics. Instructors in the 66 schools were sent a second form, a three-page questionnaire inquiring about the nature and content of their courses. Sixty-four of these forms (97 percent) were completed and returned. All instructors also included a course outline and most submitted numerous other materials, such as exams, bibliographies, and student handouts. Some 56 percent added letters or extensive comments on the back.

16. It was not too difficult to determine whether the courses offered were devoted fundamentally to ethics. Some arbitrariness was inevitable in distinguishing these courses from those with a broader intent to discuss modern issues such as the press's responsibility in a democratic society. However, in every doubtful case, the administrator's or instructor's self-designation was used as to whether this course was specifically in ethics or not. The word "ethics" provided a negative boundary. If it was in the course title, it was included—though obviously that word was not required for a course to be listed as devoted specifically to ethics. In fact, titles for these courses

varied greatly. Typical ones: "Journalism Ethics," "Law and Ethics," "Ethics and Mass Communications," "Social Responsibility of the Media," "Ethical Problems of the Press." The word "ethics" appeared in 83 percent of the course titles.

17. Textbooks preferred in media ethics courses at the time of the survey: Hulteng, *Messenger's Motives* (21 courses); Merrill-Barney, *Ethics and the Press,* and Nelson-Teeter, *Law of Mass Communications* (7 courses); Rivers-Schramm, *Responsibility in Mass Communication* (5 courses); Gross, *Responsibility of the Press,* and Francois, *Mass Media Law and Regulation,* and Gillmor-Barron, *Mass Communication Law* (3 courses). See the annotated bibliography below for details on these and other media ethics books.

18. John M. Harrison, "Media, Men, and Morality," *Review of Politics,* 36, no. 2 (April 1974), 250–64. It is beyond our purpose to engage the problem here of universal values versus those culturally conditioned. See, for example, Abraham Maslow, ed., *New Knowledge in Human Values* (New York: Harper & Row, 1959).

19. John C. Parker and Louis J. Rubin, *Process as Content: Curriculum Design and the Application of Knowledge* (Chicago: Rand McNally, 1966).

20. One respondent to an earlier draft included this provocative reaction to the claim that ethics should be taught throughout the curriculum: "I think that many such claims are self-deceiving at best and fraudulent at worst. In fact, I suspect that many reporting courses operate on principles that bar ethical considerations as unworthy." See *The Teaching of Ethics in Higher Education* (Hastings-on-Hudson, N.Y.: The Hastings Center, 1980).

21. The definition assumed here is that ethics is a liberal arts discipline which appraises voluntary human conduct in so far as it can be judged right or wrong in reference to determinative principles. Ēthos in its original Greek meaning was "sent," "haunt," "abode," "accustomed dwelling place," that is, the place from which we proceed, that from which we start out, the "home base." From *ēthos* is derived *ēthikos (plur: ta ēthika),* meaning "of or for morals." This word came to stand in the Greek philosophical tradition for the systematic study of the principles that underlie behavior.

22. See Daniel Callahan, "Qualifications for the Teaching of Ethics," in Daniel Callahan and Sissela Bok, eds., *Ethics Teaching in Higher Education* (New York: Plenum Press, 1980).

23. For a vigorous plea that journalism take philosophical ethics seriously, see James W. Carty, "Ethics: A Lost Concept," *The Collegiate Journalist* 8, no. 3 (Spring 1971): 11, 18; and his "Needed: An Ethical Perspective," *Grassroots Editor* 10, no. 1 (January–February 1969): 10–11.

24. Max Lerner, "The Shame of the Professions," *Saturday Review,* November 1, 1975, p. 11. Lerner's article introduces a special section, "What is

Happening to Ethical Standards in Government, Law, Business, Accounting, Journalism, Medicine, Education?'' pp. 12–29.

25. Obviously this list can be no better than an approximation. One cannot tell for sure how seriously the content of textbooks is taken, for example. (Incidentally, only in four courses does the textbook outline provide the course outline). A larger problem is overlapping of categories. For example, in some courses, daily newsgathering practice includes the problem of bias and fairness. Moreover, providing very general rubrics as done below tends to obscure the immense variety in specifics and procedures.

26. Daniel Callahan and Sissela Bok, eds., *Ethics Teaching in Higher Education* (New York: Plenum Press, 1980): Sissela Bok, ''Whistle-Blowing and Professional Responsibilities''; Dennis Thompson, ''Paternalism in Medicine, Law, and Public Policy.''

27. Robert Park, ''The Natural History of the Newspapers,'' *American Journal of Sociology* 29 (Nov. 1923): 273–89.

28. Quoted in Charles Seib, ''Readers Judge Newspapers,'' syndicated in *Syracuse* (N.Y.) *Post-Standard*, 5 March 1979.

29. For a summary of these issues and an extensive bibliography on privacy and journalism, see Joseph P. McKerns, ''The Private Lives of Public Officials: Can the Right of Privacy Survive the First Amendment,'' unpublished paper, University of Tennessee, 1978.

30. Karl Jaspers, *Reason and Existenz,* trans. William Earle (New York: Routledge and Kegan Paul, 1955).

31. Sissela Bok, *Lying: Moral Choice in Public and Private Life* (New York: Pantheon Books, 1978); quotation from St. Augustine, p. xv.

32. Edward J. Epstein, ''Journalism and Truth,'' *Commentary,* April 1974, pp. 36–40.

33. In one sense, this statement is too mild. Much of the basis for the press seeking greater privilege—for encouraging First Amendment exceptionalism for itself—is that the press *acts for* and *stands for* society at large. See Everette Dennis, ''The Rhetoric and Reality of Representation: A Legal Basis for Press Freedom and Minority Rights,'' in Bernard Rubin, ed., *Small Voices and Great Trumpets: Minorities and the Media* (Cambridge: Massachusetts Institute of Technology Press, in press).

34. In a letter (6/14/79), James Boylan provides a helpful classroom technique for dealing with this challenge-to-authority matter: ''I found especially useful David W. Ewing's *Freedom Inside the Organization* (New York: McGraw Hill, 1977), which does not deal specifically with journalism but discusses rights of employees in general, and particularly the right to dissent from organization policy without retribution—a right particularly important in journalism. One very telling exercise that we did was to compare Ewing's employee ''bill of rights'' with the code of professional conduct issued this year by the Philadelphia *Inquirer;* the *Inquirer,* it appeared, was clearly guilty of

claiming authority over ethical issues to which no employer, by Ewing's standards, was entitled."

35. Codes adopted by newspapers and broadcast stations and those designed for particular problem areas (riot codes, press-bar guidelines, for example) are proving to be valuable innovations. Eventually they may be able to accomplish what so far has eluded the more general codes of professional organizations. Although he has serious reservations about journalism codes, John Merrill indicates how much students benefit if they are asked as a class exercise to write a code superior to the SPJ, SDX code. For this and other suggestions on teaching media ethics, see his "Do We Teach Ethics—Or Do We Teach About Ethics," *Journalism Educator* 33, no. 2 (July 1978): 59–60.

36. William Rivers has produced two award-winning books in this area, *The Opinionmakers* (Boston: Beacon Press, 1965), and especially *The Adversaries* (Boston: Beacon Press, 1970). He correctly argues for maintaining a delicate balance between government and media, and shows particular sensitivity to the problem of the press being co-opted. Without question people must be informed if democratic government is to work, and that entails its corollary—that public officials should not themselves provide such information.

37. Cf. Everette E. Dennis, "Journalistic Primitivism," *Journal of Popular Culture* (Summer 1975), pp. 122–35. The adversary idea has often produced a frenzied pace so occupied with scandal that other political and social dimensions go unnoticed.

38. James C. Thomson, "Journalistic Ethics: Some Probings by a Media Keeper," January 1978, The Poynter Center, Indiana University, p. 10.

39. *The Teaching of Ethics in Higher Education: A Report by The Hastings Center* (Hastings-on-Hudson, N.Y.: The Hastings Center, 1980).

40. Richard A. Schwarzlose, "Socratic Method Adds Zest to Ethics, Law Classes," *Journalism Educator* 33, no. 1 (April 1978): 9–13, 24.

41. Ibid., p. 24

42. For details on working out this approach, see Clifford G. Christians, "Problem-Solving in a Mass Media Course," *Communication Education* 28, no. 2 (May 1979): 139–43.

43. Kenneth Clark, *Civilization: A Personal View* (New York: Harper & Row, 1969), p. 76.

44. For comments on the tripartite process, personal communication from Everette Dennis, March 20, 1979.

45. J. Bronowski, *The Ascent of Man* (New York: Little, Brown and Co., 1973), p. 54.

46. For two essays and an annotated list of the films that portray moral dilemmas among news people, see Bernard Rubin, ed., *Questioning Media Ethics* (New York: Praeger Special Studies, 1978), pp. 209–82.

47. H. Stuart Hughes, *History as Art and as Science* (New York: Harper & Row, 1964), pp. 6–7. The advent of television has reduced somewhat the time pressures on newspaper journalists, though deadlines continue as a vital consideration.

48. The validity of this position has been debated for the last half-century. As the result of a national study of newsmen's views and opinions, Johnstone and his associates have postulated two belief systems. The first is the neutral system which considers news as arising naturally from events, and the journalist as neutral channel. The other, that of a participant press, conceptualizes much news as arising from active participation by the journalist, who must also interpret events and place them in a meaningful context. Older journalists and those rising in the news hierarchy tend to espouse the neutral concept, Johnstone concludes, while younger professionals tend to favor the participant ideology. Those oriented to participant values appear to find the field less satisfying. Their image of professional practice appears in large part incompatible with organizational realities. In John W. C. Johnstone, Edward J. Slawski, William W. Bowman, *The News People* (Urbana, Ill.: University of Illinois Press, 1976), chaps. 7–8. For a study of socialization in the television newsroom, see Dan Garvey, "Social Control in the Television Newsroom" (Ph.D. dissertation, Stanford University, 1971), as cited in Everette Dennis, *The Media Society,* (Dubuque, Iowa: W. C. Brown Co., 1978), pp. 96–7 and 106, f.n. 16.

For the most part, news which is quickly processed and delivered with a minimum of perceivable slant or bias is more acceptable to a mass audience. The convention of "value neutrality" not only protects against the financial hazard of libel suits, but also provides more attractively neutral material for the American public and the international market. Therefore, behaviors associated with the value-neutral position are typically considered desirable. Cf. Jeremy Tunstall, *The Media Are American: Anglo-American Media in the World* (New York: Columbia University Press, 1977), pp. 201–2.

49. Unfortunately, as psychiatrist Jerome D. Frank of Johns Hopkins University notes, audiences are often caught up in the same sense of temporal continuities. "The mass media," he writes, "bombard us with news of transient events, all presented with the same air of importance regardless of long term significance." From the individual's perspective, "loss of temporal continuity weakens feelings of personal meaning and significance by undermining those features of character and personality on which those feelings depend....I keep thinking of the Doonesbury cartoon in which the television news commentator Roland Burton Hedley says, 'We'll give this issue in-depth coverage—45 seconds.'" Thus, trusting readers to provide the proper time-space location is problematical. Frank, "Mental Health in a Fragmented Society."

50. Lou Cannon, *Reporting: An Inside View* (Sacramento: California Journal Press, 1977), chap. 7. John Craig, *Pittsburgh Post-Gazette,* believes that changing patterns of competition have modified the nature of time constraints for newspaper reporters though they remain stringent in television. Personal communication May 20, 1979.

51. Louis Hodges, "Applied Ethics and Pre-Professionals," Hastings Center Paper, Oct. 1978.

52. For comments shaping the discussion of professionalism in this essay, John C. Craig, Jr., Editor, *Pittsburgh Post-Gazette,* and John McMillan, Executive Editor, Salem, *Oregon Statesman,* have been particularly helpful.

53. T. M. Scanlon argues for a two-tiered view which gives an important role to consequences and yet takes rights seriously as placing limits on consequentialist reasoning. Such a view, differing from rule utilitarianism in important ways, illustrates a possible approach. "Rights, Goals, and Fairness," *Erkenntnis,* 1977, pp. 81–95.

54. Cf. three unpublished Hastings Center papers on "What is Normative Ethics?" by Kurt Baier, Gene Outka, and Frederick Olafson, May 1978.

55. This reconstruction of Aristotle's *Nicomachean Ethics* benefits from Georg Gadamer, *Truth and Method* (New York: Seabury Press, 1975), pp. 280 ff.

56. Walter Lippmann's worry in *Public Opinion* (1922; reprinted, New York: Harcourt, Brace, 1974), p. 274. Lippmann was concerned, for example, that the press was accumulating even the responsibility reserved for the referendum. The concern that journalism have a noninflated and well-articulated place arises from Margaret Blanchard's conclusion based on a historical study of press criticism: "The Press is a social institution and...if it gets too out of line with the overall needs of the society it serves, moves will be made to return it to a role perceived as more appropriate. This has happened before and it can happen again." *Journalism History* 5, no. 2 (Summer 1978): p. 54.
A reader of an earlier version of this monograph appended this comment, a point of view which certainly needs to be confronted as the press's goals are clarified: "I disagree with the apparent premise that the press plays a powerful, all-pervasive, imperial role in the political process. In my judgment, it does not take enough responsibility and initiative. Its failings are not those of a rampant mammoth, but of a somnolent sloth, feeding on the public's apathy. In short, I think Lippmann's worries unfounded. A worse fate has unfolded."

57. The justifying principle has become so indispensable in moral theory that we can no longer assume morality to be a closed, self-authenticating system. Sissela Bok's book, *Lying,* outlines three specific steps to which our behavior must be subjected before it can be judged as moral (chap. 7).

58. Samuel Gorovitz and Bruce Miller, eds., "Professional Responsibility in the Law: A Curriculum Report from the Institute on Law and Ethics," Summer 1977, Council for Philosophical Studies, University of Maryland, College Park, Maryland.

59. Keith P. Sanders and Won H. Chang, "Freebies: Achille's Heel of Journalism Ethics," March 1977, Freedom of Information Foundation, University of Missouri.

60. Herb Altschull, "Secrecy in the Newsroom" unpublished paper, School of Journalism, Indiana University, 1978.

61. G. Norman Van Tubergen (with S. Whitlow, J. Black, R. Barney), "Journalists' Ethics: Two Qualitative Studies," unpublished paper, University of Kentucky, 1979.

62. Kim B. Rotzoll and Clifford G. Christians, "An Inquiry into Advertising Practitioners' Perceptions of Ethical Decisions: The Advertising Agency," and "Ethics in the Film Industry: A Study of Practitioners' Perceptions," unpublished papers, sponsored by the McCormick Foundation, University of Illinois-Urbana, 1979.

63. Todd Hunt, "A Study of Ethics Codes in New Jersey Daily Newspapers," Institute for Communication Studies, Rutgers University, 1977.

Bibliography

BOOKS (arranged by year of publication):

Crawford, Nelson A. *The Ethics of Journalism*. New York: Alfred A. Knopf, 1924. A commentary on the press's ethical standards, aiming to guide students and stimulate the formation of professional codes.

Flint, Leon N. *The Conscience of the Newspaper*. New York: D. Appleton, 1925. Section I introduces actual cases and gives suggestions on how the ethical problems in each should be treated. Parts II and III discuss more general difficulties inherent in the newspaper's nature and in the forces shaping its future.

Gibbons, William F. *Newspaper Ethics: A Discussion of Good Practice for Journalists*. Ann Arbor, Mich.: Edwards Bros., 1926. A mimeographed volume discussing principial questions arising from actual professional practice and arguing for the formation of professional codes and organizations.

Rivers, William L. and Schramm, Wilbur. *Responsibility in Mass Communication*. Rev. ed. New York: Harper and Row [1957], 1969. Delineates the mass media's role in modern society, takes note of various criticism, and suggests responsiblities on the part of government, public, and media.

Gerald, J. Edward. *The Social Responsibility of the Press*. Minneapolis: University of Minnesota Press, 1963. Views mass media as a social institution, attempts to evaluate how effectively they serve society, and proposes some substantive and complex improvements.

Gross, Gerald. *The Responsibility of the Press*. New York: Fleet Publishing Co., 1966. A collection of thirty-one essays, nearly all of them using "responsibility" in their titles. Written by a wide range of authors, both academics and practitioners. Covers several media—newspapers, television, books, and film—and several functions, including editing and production.

Haselden, Kyle. *Morality and the Mass Media.* Nashville: Broadman Press, 1968. Applies an enlightened Christian moral perspective to mass media content, dealing especially with censorship, sex, obscenity, commercialism, and violence.

Thayer, Lee, ed. *Communication: Ethical and Moral Issues.* New York: Gordon and Breach, 1973. Compilation of addresses given at the University of Iowa in 1969–70 by well-known academics, several of them internationals. Concludes with an attempt to sketch out the theoretical direction an ethics of communication should take.

Heine, William C. *Journalism Ethics: A Case Book.* London, Ontario: University of Western Ontario Library, 1975. Twelve cases, each one to ten pages long, gathered largely from the Britain and Ontario Press Councils. They cover such topics as advertising, invasion of privacy, secret documents, sensational photos, and the reporting of scandal.

Johannesen, Richard L. *Ethics in Human Communication.* Columbus, Ohio: Charles E. Merrill, 1975; reprinted, Wayne, N.J.: Avery Publishing Group, 1978. Outlines four perspectives within which students can make ethical judgments about communication. Very worthwhile footnotes and bibliography, though more applicable to interpersonal than to mass communication.

Merrill, John C. and Barney, Ralph, eds. *Ethics and the Press.* New York: Hastings House, 1975. A collection of articles and addresses focused on the media's news function. Part I deals with philosophical and theoretical issues; Part II presents ethical dilemmas faced in everyday newsgathering.

Hulteng, John L. *The Messenger's Motives: Ethical Problems of the News Media.* Englewood Cliffs, N.J.: Prentice-Hall, 1976. Compiles a series of cases and illustrations to show how the media operate, and investigates how successfully they live up to these guidelines which can be distilled from contemporary ethics codes and accepted practices.

Alley, Robert S. *Television: Ethics for Hire.* Nashville: Abingdon, 1977. Using extensive interviews with dozens of producers and writers for prime-time television, the author analyzes their personal values and how they are incorporated into their programs.

Casebier, Allan and Casebier, Janet J., eds. *Social Responsibility of the Mass Media.* Washington, D.C.: University Press of America, 1978. Papers and discussions from a 1976 conference at the University of Southern California where media specialists and academicians define the rights and obligations of mass media news and entertainment. The editor provides a summary chapter (8) on social responsibility.

Rubin, Bernard, ed. *Questioning Media Ethics.* New York: Praeger Special Studies, 1978. Chapters based on research projects commissioned by

Boston University's Institute for Democratic Communication. There are four general articles on the state of journalism ethics, plus coverage of specific problems such as small-town journalism, third world, advertising to children, fairness doctrine, stereotyping of women. A valuable section is included on the Hollywood films which portray journalists' moral dilemmas.

Swain, Bruce M. *Reporters' Ethics.* Ames: Iowa State University Press, 1978. A readable summary of the ethical problems faced by 67 reporters from 16 metropolitan dailies who were interviewed by the author.

The Teaching of Ethics in Higher Education: A Report by The Hastings Center. Hastings-on-Hudson, N.Y.: The Hastings Center, 1980.

Callahan, Daniel and Bok, Sissela, eds. *Ethics Teaching in Higher Education.* New York: Plenum Press, 1980.

SELECTED ARTICLES (in addition to those cited)

Anderson, David A. and Benjaminson, Peter, eds. "The Ethics of Investigative Reporting." In *Investigative Reporting.* Bloomington, Ind: Indiana University Press, 1976.

Block, Randy. "How Effective is Our Code of Ethics?" *Bulletin of the American Society of Newspaper Editors,* July 1968, pp. 1–3, 13–15.

Cheseboro, James, "A Construct for Assessing Ethics in Communication," *Central States Speech Journal* 20 (Summer 1969): 104–14.

Christians, Clifford G. "Fifty Years of Scholarship in Media Ethics," *Journal of Communication* 27 (Autumn 1977): 19–29.

———. "Problem-Solving in a Mass-Media Course," *Communication Education* 28 (May 1979): 139–43.

———. "Jacques Ellul's Concern With the Amorality of Contemporary Communications," *Communications: International Journal of Mass Communication Research,* January 1977, pp. 62–80.

"Covering Watergate: Success and Backlash," *Time,* 8 July 1974, pp. 68–75.

Diggs, Bernard J. "Persuasion and Ethics," *The Quarterly Journal of Speech* 50, no. 4 (December 1974): 359–73.

Dimmick, John. "Canons and Codes as Occupational Ideologies," *Journal of Communication* (Spring 1977): 181–87.

Drummond, William J. and Zycher, August. "Arafat's Press Agents," *Harper's,* March 1976, pp. 24–30.

Epstein, Edward Jay. "Journalism and Truth," *Commentary,* April 1974, pp. 36–40.

Gulley, Halbert. "The New Amorality in American Communication," *Today's Speech* 18, no. 1 (Winter 1970): 3–8.

Hardt, Hanno. "The Dilemma of Mass Communication: An Existential Point of View," *Philosophy and Rhetoric* 5 (Summer 1972): 175–87.

Harwood, Richard. "Newspaper Ethics: The Confusion Over Conflict of Interest," *The Quill*, July 1971, pp. 20–22.

Hentoff, Nat. "Would You Run This Ad: A Survey of Publishers," *Business and Society Review*, Summer 1975, pp. 8–13.

Hermann, Jean-Maurice. "The International Ethics of Journalists," *The Xenocratic Journalist*, December 1977, pp. 9–12.

Hickey, Neil. "Was the Truth Buried at Wounded Knee?" *TV Guide*, December 1, 8, 15, 22, 1973.

Keller, Paul W. and Brown, Charles T. "An Interpersonal Ethic for Communication," in *Messages*. Edited by Jean M. Civikly. New York: Random House, 1974.

Kelley, Frank K. "Ethics of Journalism in a Century of Change," *Nieman Reports*, 22 (June 1968): 12–15.

McCarthy, Eugene. "Sins of Omission: The Media as Censor," *Harper's*, June 1977, pp. 90–92.

McKerns, Joseph P. "Media Ethics: A Bibliographical Essay," *Journalism History* 5, no. 2 (Summer 1978): 50–53, 68.

Persky, Joel. "Self-Regulation of Broadcasting—Does It Exist?" *Journal of Communication* (Spring 1977): 202–10.

Ryan, Kevin. "Television as a Moral Educator," in *Television as a Cultural Force*. Edited by Richard Adler. New York: Praeger, 1976.

Sanders, Keith P. and Chang, Won H. "Codes—the Ethical Free For All: A Survey of Journalists' Opinions About Freebies," Columbia, Mo.: Freedom of Information Foundation, 1977.

Shorris, Earl. "Cutting Velvet at the *New York Times*," *Harper's*, October 1977, pp. 102–10.

Siepmann, Charles A. "What is Wrong With TV—and With Us," in *The Range of Ethics*. Edited by Richard A. Wright. New York: American Book Co., 1966.

Slaby, Ronald, et al. "Television Violence and Its Sponsors," *Journal of Communication* (Winter 1976): 88–96.

Stern, Laurence. "The Daniel Schorr Affair: A Morality Play for the Fourth Estate," *Columbia Journalism Review* (May–June, 1976): 20–25.

Wieman, Henry N. and Walter, Otis M. "Toward an Analysis of Ethics for Rhetoric," *Quarterly Journal of Speech* 43, no. 3 (October 1957): 266–70.

Witcover, Jules, "William Loeb and the New Hampshire Primary: A Question of Ethics," *Columbia Journalism Review* 21 (May–June 1972): 14–25.

Publications from The Teaching of Ethics Project
The Hastings Center

A number of publications on the teaching of ethics in higher education are available from The Hastings Center. A list of these publications appears on the back cover. Return order form to: The Hastings Center, 360 Broadway, Hastings-on-Hudson, N.Y. 10706

I. **The Teaching of Ethics in Higher Education: A Report by The Hastings Center** .... ($5) _____
II. Michael J. Kelly, Legal Ethics and Legal Education .... ($4) _____
III. Clifford G. Christians & Catherine L. Covert, Teaching Ethics in Journalism Education .... ($4) _____
IV. K. Danner Clouser, Teaching Bioethics: Strategies, Problems, and Resources .... ($4) _____
V. Charles W. Powers & David Vogel, Ethics in the Education of Business Managers. .... ($5) _____
VI. Donald P. Warwick, The Teaching of Ethics in the Social Sciences. .... ($4) _____
VII. Robert J. Baum, Ethics and Engineering Curricula. .... ($4) _____
VIII. Joel L. Fleishman & Bruce L. Payne, Ethical Dilemmas and the Education of Policymakers .... ($4) _____
IX. Bernard Rosen & Arthur C. Caplan, Ethics in the Undergraduate Curriculum. .... ($4) _____

TOTAL COST _____

PRICES QUOTED ARE POSTPAID—
PREPAYMENT IS REQUIRED
There will be a $1 service charge
if billing is necessary.

Name _____

Address _____

City _____ State _____ Zip Code _____